cook like a rock star

cook like a rock star

125 Recipes, Lessons, and Culinary Secrets

ANNE BURRELL

with Suzanne Lenzer
FOREWORD BY MARIO BATALI

Photographs by Ben Fink

CLARKSON POTTER/PUBLISHERS
NEW YORK

Published in the United States by Clarkson
Potter/Publishers, an imprint of the Crown
Publishing Group, a division of Random
House, Inc., New York.

www.crownpublishing.com
www.clarksonpotter.com

CLARKSON POTTER is a trademark and
POTTER with colophon is a registered
trademark of Random House, Inc.

Library of Congress Cataloging-in-
Publication Data is available
upon request

ISBN 978-0-307-88675-0

Printed in China

DESIGN BY Laura Palese
JACKET DESIGN BY Jane Treuhaft
JACKET FRONT PHOTOGRAPH BY Ben Fink

10 9 8 7 6 5 4 3 2 1

First Edition

FOR
MY MOM

THE ORIGINAL FREE SPIRIT
FROM WHOM I DERIVE
MY STRENGTH, PASSION,
CREATIVITY & WINGS.

CONTENTS

ACKNOWLEDGMENTS 8

FOREWORD BY MARIO BATALI 10

INTRODUCTION 12

1
PICCOLINI
(a.k.a. my little nibbles)

23

2
FIRSTS
(the introduction)

61

3
PASTA
(my passion)

99

4
SECONDS
(the main event)

143

5
SIDES
(the sparkle factor)

189

6
DESSERTS
(my sweeties!)

221

INDEX 252

ACKNOWLEDGMENTS

There are so people in so many parts of my life—both professionally and personally—that have helped to make this book possible. Thank you all SOOOOO much!

My family: MARLENE, JANE, BEN, JIM, AND, OF COURSE, THEIR FAMILIES. You guys are my roots and rocks. You provide the love, laughter, and support that helps make me who I am. I love you all.

CHRISTINA CAIN, an amazing friend and sous chef who has been there through thick and thin, always with unwavering loyalty, support, and a smile. You are truly a special person.

My mentor, MARIO BATALI, you are the reason I am where I am today. Thank you for all your generosity, advice, and support along the way.

SCOTT FELDMAN, as both my manager and my friend, thank you for everything you do (and for putting up with me!).

DANIELLE FINE, the glue that holds so many things together. I love working with you.

SUZANNE LENZER, the amazing writer who captured my voice, channeled my energy, and kept me on track with delightfulness.

JANIS DONNAUD, my agent, who thankfully took me on and has been a lot of fun to work with.

REYNA MASTROSIMONE, JULIET DANNIBILE, and SHEENA TRACEY, the amazing friends who keep me grounded and smiling. I am so lucky to have such a great group of girls in my life.

PHIL CASACELI, the keeper of my local and a great friend.

JAMES KUHNER and DEACON CARPENTER, friends who have become family and who helped me invent "piccolini."

BEN FINK, GARY NOEL, JEFF KAVANAUGH, JAMIE KIMM, and DANI FISHER, the creative group of people responsible for the images in this book.

CESARE CASELLA, MARK LADNER, ROBERTO TREVINO, ALEX GUARNASCHELLI, BOBBY FLAY, and MICHAEL SYMON—the very talented group of chefs who I am proud to call friends.

EMILY TAKOUDES and CLARKSON POTTER— my wonderful editor and the publishing house that gave me the opportunity to put my voice onto paper.

Everyone at the FOOD NETWORK for believing in me and giving me a platform to reach so many people. Thank you for giving me a chance. Especially my team at the Food Network: SHELLEY HOFFMAN, SARAH PAULSEN, MARK DISSIN, MIKE SCHEAR, SUSAN STOCKTON, YOUNG SUN HUH, and the Food Network Kitchens. You people have allowed my dream to become a reality.

VINCENT OQUENDO, my make-up artist. The one who makes me look pretty and who has LOTS of lashes!

MS. MARNI, the truly talented seamstress who makes my skirts and dresses me in all the pretty colors!

JEFF LIEB, my stage manager, and the inspiration behind many of my one-liners.

FOREWORD BY

I have known and cooked with Anne Burrell for more than fifteen years and have always known that she was ready for prime time. I cannot remember a dish of food that she ever made that left me anything but purely satisfied.

We first worked together at a wine store. My partner there at the time was a bitter tyrant who was her boss. Every day he would throw bad attitude curve balls at her and yet she was still capable of creating delicious food and purveying a relaxed and joyous feeling about food and Italian culture that made everyone who walked in feel happy. Her resolute and firm belief in the adage that real food in a real setting will calm and soothe both the palate and the person was the heart and soul of first her kitchen, then the staff, and eventually the whole store and its myriad customer base. When it came time to choose players in my very first *Iron Chef America* I really did not

have to think twice about Anne being on the team. We went to L.A. and met the original masters, competed first against Morimoto and then with Chef Sakai against Bobby and Morimoto in an odd sound studio, and Anne fell for Sakai like a ton of bricks.

Anne could cook, she could take the heat, and she had a good time. All three still ring true. I do not think anyone in New York was quite prepared for the thrilling and thoughtful food Anne first presented at Centro Vinoteca when it opened in 2007. Her casual yet serious food became a true trademark, particularly the category of small tapas-style antipasti called piccolini. Here Anne really got the traction she deserved in the world of YUM and the place became the San Juan Capistrano for foodie swallows around the country as the faithful found a place to worship at Anne's culinary altar. We continued as a team and as friends

MARIO BATALI

through four seasons of *Iron Chef* and worked the teamwork and work ethic components to yield a pretty great record in kitchen stadium. Of course the smart folks at Food Network fell in love with Anne in the studio and have since groomed her to be the Big Thing on air. She has a couple of fun showcases for her irreverent brand of food smarts and playful innuendo that works perfectly in the post-modern world of hybrid food competition and information programming that has become the new hallmark in the food space. I imagine she will have a long and successful TV career into the future. Maybe I could lure her back into a restaurant kitchen!

In the absence of a place to pull up a bar stool and taste her creative and lusty dishes, this book steps in to fill the gap. Now I can steal her food (like I have for years on *Iron Chef*) and make it at my own home. The piccolini are simply delicious and easy to make, and a series of three or four of them could easily become a casual breezy meal in no time. The legendary pasta, the same "noodles" she has made on *Iron Chef,* can now effortlessly become part of your repertoire and you can wow your friends with your Italian know-how and kiss kiss–ciao baby way in the kitchen. Anne breaks down each of her recipes into easy to understand *mise en place* and then technical steps that reduce complicated-sounding dishes to a level that even a novice cook can make. All of this is presented in her voice, one that you can hear on your mind's TV, coaxing the cook in you forward through these dishes to the ultimate and tasty finish. Like Anne, this book is fun, easy to understand, and ultimately delicious. Like Anne, there is more to this book than the simple layout and recklessly trick-free recipes. *Cook Like a Rock Star* is tasty happiness and ready for the party.

INTRODUCTION

YOU ARE THE CHEF
OF YOUR OWN KITCHEN.
ROCK IT OUT!

....

People say that chefs are the new rock stars. That's why I named this book *Cook Like a Rock Star*. Because YOU are the chef of your own kitchen—so you are a rock star too.

Being a rock star in the kitchen means taking control, having fun, and thinking of cooking as entertainment. Yes, dinner is entertainment, but I want to help you make the process of *making dinner* entertainment too. This book is about empowering you to own what you do in your kitchen, to be excited by what you're making, and to experience the same kind of joy that I feel every day when I cook.

It doesn't matter who you are, what size or shape you are, what day of the week it is. If you whip up a quick meal from scratch that you're proud of, rather than just open up a container or pull a tub out of the fridge, then you, my friend, are a rock star. Own it and have fun!

....

MY MISSION IS TO HELP YOU MAKE DINNER—TONIGHT!

Cooking is not a genetically inherited skill—people forget this. Just because your mom or your grandma is a good cook doesn't mean you will be. Cooking is something that you need to *learn* how to do—just like everything else. The purpose of this book is to teach you how, in a fun way, to cook—or to help you expand your skills and your repertoire if you're already comfy in the kitchen.

When I was in grade school, high school, even college, I just wasn't interested in school; I did as little as I could to get by. But when I went to culinary school, it was all about doing and using my hands—not just listening. I was like a sponge. Finally, I was in the right place at the right time in my life; I actually enjoyed school and *wanted* to learn. And that's my goal with this book: to get you cooking and tasting things and having so much fun you don't even realize how much you're learning.

I went to culinary school to learn how to cook and I've been working for years to know all that I do today—but I'm going to leapfrog you ahead. I'm giving you the benefit of my blood, sweat, tears, and even my mistakes in this book. But I'm also giving you my happiness and joy—my triumphs!

As a girl who has spent most of her career in restaurant kitchens and as a culinary teacher, cooking is part of my soul. For years I've been internalizing cooking techniques, losing sleep over them, and forever fantasizing about food. I've learned how to coax the most out of a dish, how to combine ingredients to get the best flavor, and how to time everything so it all comes together at the moment it should. I've

worked hard to become the cook that I am, and I'm proud to call myself a chef. But chefs aren't rocket scientists, and most of what we do is not all that difficult. It's stuff you can do at home once you know how—which is what I want to teach you with this book . . . and we're going to have A LOT of fun along the way.

The recipes in this book are very near and dear to me, and they get me excited every time I look at them. (Even while I was writing this book, I'd sometimes stop and think, "This sounds SOOOOO good, I want to make this now!") This collection tells the story of who I am as a chef, and if you take these recipes and make them your own, they'll help you develop your inner chef too (a.k.a. your inner rock star).

So here's the dealio: I want you to have fun making dinner tonight, and then I want you to sit down with your husband, wife, boyfriend, girlfriend, kids, closest friends, first date, neighbors down the hall, anyone, and eat the delicious meal that you made—from scratch—yourself. I want you to know what it feels like to create lovely food for people you care about and feel confident that you can do it over and over again. I want you to rock out and be the chef of your own kitchen! And I want to help you do it.

THE MAKING OF A GIRL CHEF

Apparently I started on my journey toward becoming a chef at a very early age. According to my mother, when I was three years old I came to her and said, "I have a friend named Julie," and she asked, "You do? Julie who?" And I said, "Julie Child! I watch her every day on TV." It was another twenty years before I had the epiphany that led me to make cooking my career, but even as a kid I knew that dinner—making dinner—could be fun.

When I started out in the food world, there weren't many women in restaurant kitchens, and the Food Network was in its infancy. I started cooking because I was totally passionate about food—the concept of celebrity chefs didn't even exist yet! I went to culinary school because I wanted to know everything I could about food and become a badass cook. All I wanted to do was work in a restaurant.

After graduating from the Culinary Institute of America, I did a second stint at a culinary school in Italy to learn how to cook Italian food. My time in Italy opened my eyes to a whole other world of food, cooking, and a way of life that I didn't even know existed. When I got back to the States, I headed straight to New York City—where I'd always wanted to end up—and I was immediately drawn to Lidia Bastianich, the owner and chef of Felidia. I wanted to work for her because I had worked with several women in Italy and it felt like a natural progression to do so back home. I also wanted to learn all I could from someone I respected. I watched how she handled herself, her staff, and her food, and I learned a lot about how to be a girl chef in what is still mostly a man's world (kitchen). And I learned that I liked being one of the only girls in the boys' club!

From the very beginning of my career, my mantra was, "I will work harder than any guy; I will stay later and be better than anyone. And no guy is ever going to have to pick up a stockpot for me!" So I worked like crazy to prove myself. You have to be tough in a professional kitchen—playing with fire and knives is dangerous, and I do it wearing a skirt and a smile. I feel very lucky to have found my passion and I love the path I've chosen. I can go anywhere in the world and do my job. I love the people who work in restaurants—they're intelligent, creative, and have a different take on life. And my education is never over. In this business there's always something new to learn.

LOOK AT YOU, BECOMING A CHEF!

Being a chef is a matter of having a good basic foundation—an understanding of the principles and techniques of cooking. Sure, there's talent involved, but the majority of it is simply learning the process, knowing the techniques, and practicing them over and over again until they're ingrained in your being. Cooking is about learning what to look for, what to listen for, how a dish should smell, how it should feel, and, of course, what it should taste like—you use all your senses when you cook and those are tools that we all have at our disposal; we just need to use them.

For the home cook, it's not so important to know a bunch of culinary terminology. So I'm going to skip a lot of the technical kitchen terms and put everything into everyday language so it makes sense and becomes part of your daily existence in the kitchen. For example, a recipe might tell you to brown a piece of meat and then deglaze the "fond." But what the hell is "fond"? It's the crud on the bottom of the pan—the flavor, the stuff you want to scrape up and use to develop your rich brown food! By ditching the fancier cooking terms and speaking in plain English, I'm going to help you to understand *why* you brown the crap out of things (because brown food tastes good), and *how* to get the crud off the bottom of the pan (deglazing).

I'm simplifying everything here because I want you to cook! If you're new to cooking, I want to help you get over the fear factor and bump up the fun factor. If you're someone who already cooks, then I want to share some of my hard-learned lessons with you so you feel even more empowered at the stove. I have a little saying: Food is like a dog; it smells fear. If you're nervous, scared, or bunched up when you're cooking, your food will sense it. But if you embrace cooking with a sense of confidence and an air of fun, your food will taste SOOOOO much better. If you change a recipe, the recipe police are NOT going to be on their way over. If you want to use three cloves of garlic instead of one, knock yourself out. What I offer you here are my opinions as a professional chef. You can take them or leave them (but I recommend you take them).

A FEW WORDS ON RECIPES (AND WHY YOU SHOULD READ THEM BEFORE YOU COOK!)

Have you ever had a dinner party and told everyone to come over at seven, but you didn't sit down to eat until ten because dinner wasn't ready? I have, and it wasn't because I was running fashionably late. It was because I was making braised short ribs and hadn't read my recipe ahead of time. I didn't realize how long those guys had to cook. The result was a tipsy group of friends hoovering down a delicious dinner that no one even tasted because it was

so late, and everyone was tired and ready to go home by the time it was ready. All my effort was in vain because I hadn't read the recipe.

Or, have you ever been happily cooking along, excited to taste your amazing creation and call yourself a rock star, only to get to the part of a recipe that says "add the remaining flour," and you think, uh-oh, *what remaining flour*? This is something that can easily be avoided if you read the recipe first and have an understanding of where you're headed.

Whenever anybody asks me for tips for the home cook, I crack myself up because the first thing I say is, "You have to read the recipe." That's exactly what my mother used to tell me to do—and I never did. So now when I'm teaching, I can't help but hear her voice telling me to read the recipe. As much as I love my mother, I hate it that she's always right. Whether you've been cooking your entire life or are just getting into it, reading a recipe is really important; and it's amazing how it can help you prevent mistakes and frustration later on.

I've spent a lot of time writing recipes in my career and I work hard to make sure that they work, and work well—for cooks of all levels. With all of these recipes I've used what I call my "crap detector" to eliminate unnecessary steps, streamline the operation, simplify the process, and maximize the flavor. Look at me, always thinking!

DON'T MESS WITH MY *MISE EN PLACE*

Okay, so I said no fussy words, and then I start with something that does sound sort of intimidating (or at least French). That's because there's always an exception in cooking—accept it and move on. The exception here is *mise en place*, which translates to "put in place." It means get all of your prep work done before you start cooking. You'll notice that the recipes in this book are not written by ingredients and then method like most books. Instead they start with *mise en place*—your prep work—and then the recipe is broken down into numbered steps. This is how I cook and how professionals cook, and it's how you should cook, too. It doesn't matter if you're a four-star chef or a beginning home cook, you need to have your *mise en place* ready before you start cooking.

You have no idea how many times I have heard people complain that they were halfway through a recipe and realized the container of bread crumbs was almost empty or that they needed a cup of sugar and had only a quarter cup left. This is when things start to run amok and cooks start to get creative (Can I substitute bread for bread crumbs? I wonder if confectioners' sugar would work instead of regular sugar?). Take your *mise en place* seriously and you won't have to take chances with creative solutions that may or may not work.

So before you even think of turning on the stove, smash your garlic, dice your onions, wash your lettuce, and separate your eggs. Get out all your equipment so that you can just get in there and cook like a rock star. Good *mise en place* makes cooking less stressful (it also cuts down on clutter—you can clean as you go) and a lot more fun.

TASTE & SEASON AS YOU GO (A.K.A. DITCHING THE "I-HOPE-IT-COMES-OUT-ALL-RIGHT" METHOD OF COOKING)

As a chef, I make my living cooking for other people, and that includes seasoning their food for them. After years of practice, I have a very good idea of what a dish will taste like when it's done, but I would never, ever think of waiting until the end of the cooking process to taste it. You MUST taste as you go. FOOD SHOULD TASTE GOOD! If it doesn't, there's something wrong and the only way to know is to *taste it*. For some reason, home cooks have a tendency to not taste their food during the cooking process—then they wonder why it doesn't taste delicious when it's done. I call this the "I-hope-it-comes-out-all-right" method of cooking, and it doesn't work. Your palate is a muscle, and like any muscle, you need to train it. You know how you train it? Taste your food.

SALE & PEPE (SALT & PEPPER) ARE NOT MARRIED, THEY'RE ONLY DATING

I'm going to jump right out there and say this: If you don't cook with salt, you will NEVER be a good cook. Salt is a flavor enhancer; it makes things taste like what they are. Have you ever heard of someone putting salt on watermelon? And there's always a pinch of salt in desserts. Salt is not something to be scared of. If you cook from scratch with good-quality, fresh ingredients—meaning seasonal produce and high-quality meat—and you steer clear of prepared, processed, frozen, canned, and of course fast food, then you can salt your cooking with reckless abandon. As a home cook you'll never get close to using the amount of salt found in most processed and packaged foods.

Pepper, on the other hand, is not a flavor enhancer. It's a very strong spice and it adds ANOTHER flavor to food. That's why I use pepper as an ingredient. I would never think to salt and *horseradish* everything, and I treat pepper the same way. I find when people are inexperienced in the kitchen they're scared of salt, yet they go hog-wild with pepper. But Sale (sall-ay) and Pepe (Italian for salt and pepper) are not married. They are only dating. Sale makes the party; she's the life of the party. But Pepe isn't usually invited to my party—he's too strong, so I tend to leave him home. He's invited only when I want his strong personality around.

THE SPICES OF LIFE

Just because you buy spices and herbs in the same aisle of the grocery store does not make them the same thing. Dried herbs to me are gross. If you smell them, you'll know instantly that they are nothing like their fresh counterparts. I'd rather cook with no herbs than dried herbs. Dried thyme smells like dirt. Dried parsley flakes smell like something from the lawnmower bag. Dried chives are just sad, and dried basil has nothing to do with summer. Adding these ingredients to your food will not improve it, so here's my advice: Don't.

Spices, on the other hand, are an ENTIRELY different story. They are transporting, exotic, aromatic, and sexy! They're seeds, they're bark, they're pods! The world of spices is amazing and seductive, and these ingredients can add so much to your cooking—but they have to be treated with respect.

Spices should be replaced annually, so buy them in small amounts and use them regularly.

I also recommend buying spices in their whole form—for example, cumin, fennel, and coriander seeds. To use them: Toast the spices in their whole form in a dry sauté pan for three or four minutes or until they're very aromatic. Then grind them in a spice grinder. (A spice grinder is nothing more than a coffee bean grinder dedicated solely to spices—it's worth the investment and will make a world of difference in your cooking.)

I LOOOOOVE NUTS

Like spices, toasting nuts is an essential step if you want to bring out their full flavor. Some people toast nuts in a sauté pan, but they don't toast evenly this way—that's why I'm an oven toaster. Put your nuts on a baking sheet and toast them in a 350°F oven. How long does it take nuts to toast? Just long enough to forget. Start with 6 to 7 minutes, but keep an eye on them. I've spent a lot of time in my career burning nuts. Once you start to smell them it's too late—so set a timer!

What does toasting nuts do? It's just like making toast! It makes them browner, crunchier, and far more flavorful. If you feel like toasting nuts ahead, go for it, then store them in the freezer until you're ready to use them or for up to six months.

MY FAVORITE TOOLS (AND WHY I LOVE THEM)

To this day, whenever I go into a kitchen supply store I still get turned on by all the wooden spoons, bowls, and other cool tools. I just want to buy everything because having the right equipment makes cooking so much easier and more fun. Of course, there are some tools that I love more than others, and there are definitely some that I use more often. To get set up with a basic toolkit, consider this list of my personal favorites. You can always add, but start with some of these essentials. You'll begin to keep a wish list if you don't have one already, because the more you cook, the more you're going to want cool kitchen stuff!

BASIC KNIVES
Chef's knife, boning knife, paring knife, and serrated knife

WOODEN SPOONS
Lots of them!

RUBBER SPATULAS
Large and small and definitely heatproof

BENCH SCRAPE
Useful for transporting little things from one place to another, scraping, cutting dough, and cleaning up

BOWLS
Mixing bowls of various sizes

MICROPLANE
A superfine grater

FOOD MILL
Great for passing tomatoes. A food mill lets all the big-money stuff fall through and leaves the seeds and stems uptown. Also great for mashed potatoes or anything you need to purée.

FISH SPATULA
A flexible metal spatula with large holes and a sharp edge

BOX GRATER

COLANDER

MEASURING CUPS
Dry and wet

MEASURING SPOONS

MESH STRAINER

MISE EN PLACE CONTAINERS
Various shapes, sizes, and colors (they're cute!)

SALT CELLAR
A salt dish. Don't try to cook with a salt shaker!

SPIDER
A wire scooper to get things out of hot liquid easily

SPOONS
Large metal ones, with and without holes

TONGS

WHISKS
Big and small

PANS
· Large and small sauté pan with curved edges
· Large, straight-sided sauté pan
· Pasta or stockpot—a large, deep pot with a lid
· Straight-sided, wide shallow pot with a lid

· Large and small nonstick sauté pans
· Various sized saucepans with lids
· Baking sheets

FOOD PROCESSOR

IMMERSION BLENDER
For puréeing right in the pan

ELECTRIC MIXER

SPICE GRINDER
A.k.a. a coffee grinder used for spices only

KITCHEN SHEARS

PARCHMENT PAPER

SILICONE MAT

PASTRY BAGS
Disposable ones (or just use zip-top plastic bags)

TWINE

JAPANESE MANDOLINE
For slicing ingredients super-thin (use with caution, respectfully and lovingly!)

"THANK YOU FOR COMING" BOWL
A trash receptacle within arms' reach so you don't have to go back and forth to the garbage all the time.

MY BASIC PANTRY

Setting up your pantry is a bit of an investment. I know that cooking at home is supposed to be cheaper than eating out, but like anything, you need the right supplies to get started. (If you're going to play golf, you have to buy golf clubs, right?) Once you get yourself squared away with some high-quality basics, the cost of cooking goes down exponentially (and when you're cooking with good stuff and enjoying it, the fun factor goes up!). Here's a list of what I keep in my pantry all the time. Of course, you don't have to go out and buy all of this at once, but this list gives you an idea of what you ultimately want to see when you open your cupboard. Start with the things you'll use the most often and build from there. With some or all of this on hand, you can whip up a delicious meal anytime.

EXTRA VIRGIN OLIVE OIL

KOSHER SALT

BACON OR PANCETTA
(or both)

FRESH PARMIGIANO

GARLIC

ONIONS
(BTW, when I say onions, I'm referring to onions about the size of a tangerine)

CRUSHED RED PEPPER

BAY LEAVES

DRIED PASTA
(some short, some long)

RISOTTO RICE
(Arborio or Carnaroli)

POLENTA

DRIED LENTILS

CHICKEN STOCK

CANNED BEANS
(cannellini, chickpeas, and black beans)

CANNED TOMATOES

NUTS
(almonds, pine nuts, and walnuts)

RED WINE VINEGAR

BALSAMIC VINEGAR

DRIED PORCINI MUSHROOMS

TOMATO PASTE

DIJON MUSTARD

BREAD CRUMBS

CAPERS

CORIANDER SEEDS

FENNEL SEEDS

PIMENTÓN
(smoked paprika)

ANCHOVIES

CORNICHONS

TABASCO SAUCE

UNSALTED BUTTER

EGGS

MILK

FLOUR

SUGAR
(white and brown)

BAKING POWDER

BAKING SODA

HORSERADISH

TUNA FISH

KETCHUP

MAYONNAISE

SOY SAUCE

SAMBAL OELEK
(Vietnamese chili sauce)

SRIRACHA
(Asian hot sauce)

A FEW WORDS ON FANCY WORDS

Like I said, I'm not big on fussy language, but there are a few terms and Anne-isms that will help you follow my recipes.

BIG FAT FINISHING OIL
This is your big-money extra virgin olive oil, the good stuff. Heat changes the flavor of olive oil, so this is the oil you want to use when you're after a pristine, green, olive-y flavor to drizzle on pasta, salads, soups, or anything really, just before serving. There are tons of different kinds of olive oil, so experiment with them. You may want to have different big fat finishing oils for different purposes—play around and decide which ones you like best.

BIG MEAT
Any big hunk of meat, usually red meat or game.

BRAISE
A technique for cooking tough cuts of meat low and slow in liquid.

BROWN FOOD
What you get when you take the time to sear meat really well and establish big brown flavor and color.

BTB, RTS
Bring to a boil, reduce to a simmer. To reduce to a simmer you must first bring your pot to a boil—you can never turn the heat down if it hasn't gone up!

CINCHY
Easy.

CRUD
The delicious brown bits on the bottom of the pan that help develop deep, rich, meaty flavors.

DIPPER
A dipping sauce.

EQUATORIALLY
Through the middle widthwise, like the equator!

FORK-TENDER
When something can easily be pierced with a fork and meets no resistance; how you know it's fully cooked.

HOMOGENEOUS
When things are uniformly combined.

LARDONS
Sliced bacon cut crosswise into ¼-inch lengths.

MISE EN PLACE
French for "put in place." Means getting all your prep work done BEFORE you start cooking.

PICCOLINI
My teeny, tiny small plates; super-yummy, bite-size nibbles. Kind of like Italian tapas.

POC
Piece of cake, totally easy.

QC
Quality control, tasting to make sure everything is delicious.

Q&E
Quick & easy, the way we like to roll!

SAUTÉ
A quick cooking method in a "sauté pan" over high heat with a small amount of oil.

SHOOTIN' MATCH
The whole thing, whatever it is.

SOFFRITTO
A combination of veggies (usually onions, carrot, celery, and garlic) puréed to a coarse paste in a food processor. The base for braised things.

SPRINKEY-DINK
A little sprinkle.

SUPER-SECRET FLAVOR WEAPON
An ingredient that adds amazing flavor to a dish.

SWEATING
To sauté without adding any color (e.g., cook onions until they're translucent but not brown—guess what? You're sweating!).

TECHNIQUE
An approach or a method, not a specific recipe (e.g., sauté).

ROCKING OUT
LIKE A CHEF

Thinking ahead, taking your *mise en place* seriously, streamlining the process, being organized, and multitasking: These are some of the most important things you need to know—and keep in mind—to be a good home cook. It's a process. Of course you're going to screw up sometimes; all cooks do (and if they tell you they don't, they're lying). But you learn a lot from your mistakes. You learn what not to do and how to prevent it next time. You may even figure out how to fix it! Once you start to think about all this as you cook, you'll be thinking like a chef—then you'll start *feeling* like a chef. The next thing you know, you'll *cook* like a chef. Remember, YOU are the chef of your own kitchen! Way to go, rock star!!!

CH №. *1*

PICCOLINI

{ a.k.a. my little nibbles }

I love to graze, to nibble on what I call "picky" food: itty-bitty morsels made up of different flavors and textures, delicious bite-size snacks in cute servings. That's why I created what I call "piccolini." In Italian, *piccolini* means teeny, tiny—which perfectly describes my style of lovely little bites. My piccolini are small plates to be eaten with a big glass of wine (or two!) as an intro to dinner. Think of them as Italian tapas.

I STARTED MAKING PICCOLINI SERIOUSLY when I was the chef at Centro Vinoteca in New York City because I wanted to share a special tradition with my customers. These days, many of our families are made up of people we're not related to at all—friends who support us, care about us, and are there whenever we need them. My surrogate family is a group of friends I couldn't live without—most important, Jim and Deacon. We help each other through work crises and personal dramas, we get together to celebrate the good times—and of course we spend a lot of time just laughing. For years, every Friday night our little group would meet up, sometimes pretty late, for what we called our "family dinners."

Just like a family get-together, we'd meet at a restaurant to eat, drink, catch up on the week, and find out what was going on in everyone's lives. We'd always have a lot of wine and then suddenly be totally starving, at which point we'd say to the waiter, "Three orders of croquettes—STAT!" Within minutes, three plates would arrive: gorgeous little fried bites, tasty snacks that were far yummier than diving into the breadbasket and that got us excited for dinner, more wine, and, of course, more gossip and laughter.

These family dinners meant so much to me, and this ritual was such an integral part of those nights, that I wanted to re-create a similar experience at my restaurant. I wanted everyone to be able to walk in, have a drink, and start tasting good things right away, even if they weren't ready to dig in to a big meal yet. I figured, if I like to eat this way, why wouldn't my customers? But I didn't want to offer just a couple of snacks; I wanted to commit to this idea, this concept of having lots of lovely little nibbles to choose from. So I developed a separate menu of just piccolini— beautiful little bites of food designed to take the edge off while you have a drink, to get your palate going for the main course, or to make up an entire meal. As someone who loves food and tasting a variety of different things, offering lots of small plates made perfect sense to me—so I did it.

These piccolini recipes are some of my very favorites, the ones that I make over and over again and never get tired of eating—or cooking. When I make piccolini for friends, I make an assortment and serve them as a little family of flavors. Some are very easy to pull together while others take a bit of effort, but the main thing is they give you a reason to chat and drink, and they get you warmed up for what's next!

If you're making a few different piccolini, keep in mind how important variety is. Remember, always look at the big picture when you're cooking and think about how different foods work together. You want each piccolini to offer something a little different in your mouth: a bit of crunch contrasted with something smooth, maybe something salty next to something sweet. But most important, you want to have fun! Invite a few friends over, open a bottle of wine or two, and pick a bunch of your favorite piccolini.

Mortadella Pâté

Zucchini & Parm Fritters with Spicy Tomato Sauce

Stir-Fried Marinated Olives

Truffled Deviled Eggs

Figs Stuffed with Gorgonzola & Walnuts

Chicken Liver Pâté with Balsamic Onions

Peperonata with Goat Cheese

Sausage & Pancetta Stuffed Mushrooms

Oyster Mushroom Chips

Eggplant Cakes with Ricotta

Prosciutto-Arugula Breadstick "Brooms"

Polpettini (Yummy Little Meatballs)

Hard Polenta Cakes with Taleggio & Cherry Tomatoes

Parmigiano-Crusted Cauliflower with Garlic Dipper

Cipolline Tempura with Aïoli

White Bean Purée with Prosciutto

Grilled Corn, Bacon & Chili Crostini

Tomato-Basil Bruschetta

Baked Ricotta with Rosemary & Lemon

MORTADELLA PÂTÉ

Mortadella is a super-high-quality baloney. In fact, it's probably the most delicious baloney you've ever had. At one of my dinner parties I was serving mortadella and one of my guests said, "Hey, this baloney has nuts in it!" And it does: Mortadella is full of pistachios and chunky bits of fat, both of which make it super-flavorful. My mortadella pâté is puréed, mixed with whipped cream, and topped with pistachios—think of it as baloney mousse.

MISE EN PLACE

2 tablespoons unsalted butter

2 tablespoons all-purpose flour

½ cup chicken stock (see page 85)

½ pound mortadella, 6 ounces cut into 2-inch chunks and 2 ounces cut into small dice

1 cup heavy cream, whipped to medium peaks

½ cup shelled and chopped pistachios

1 Melt the butter in a large, deep saucepan. Whisk in the flour and cook for 3 to 4 minutes, continuing to whisk until well combined; it should look like wet sand. Add the chicken stock and continue to cook for another 3 to 5 minutes. Remove from the heat and set aside.

2 Purée the large chunks of mortadella in a food processor until very smooth, then add the butter-flour mixture and continue puréeing until the mixture is homogeneous. Scrape down the sides of the food processor and check the consistency—it should be very smooth.

3 Transfer the purée to a large mixing bowl and add the diced mortadella, along with a third of the whipped cream. Gently combine the whipped cream into the mixture; repeat twice more. What you're looking for is a homogeneous mixture without any streaks of cream. Transfer the pâté to a serving dish and sprinkle with pistachios.

Mmmmm . . . it's a baloney cloud!

ZUCCHINI & PARM FRITTERS

WITH SPICY TOMATO SAUCE

SERVES: 6 TO 8 · TIME: ABOUT 45 MINUTES

Everybody likes fried food (if you say you don't, you're lying!), and these little guys are fried food done beautifully: a ton of zucchini held together by just a little bit of batter. They're the perfect combination of salty, crispy, cheesy, and spicy all rolled into one. And, they're a cinch to make: Do all your *mise en place* ahead of time; then you can make the sauce and the batter at the same time. Once you're prepped, fry these babies until they're really dark and crunchy. What we want here is crispy, crunchy, and dark. Woo-hoo!

MISE EN PLACE

FOR THE SAUCE

Extra virgin olive oil

1 onion, cut into ½-inch dice

Large pinch of crushed red pepper

Kosher salt

2 cloves garlic, smashed and chopped

1 28-ounce can San Marzano tomatoes (with their juices), passed through a food mill or puréed

FOR THE FRITTERS

Extra virgin olive oil

2 onions, cut into ½-inch dice

Kosher salt

1 zucchini, cut into ½-inch dice

½ cup all-purpose flour

½ cup freshly grated Parmigiano, plus more for garnish

1 teaspoon baking powder

¼ to ½ cup whole milk

Peanut or other neutral-flavored oil

FOR THE SAUCE

1 Coat a large saucepan with olive oil, add the onion and a decent pinch of red pepper—don't go crazy here with the spicy stuff, you can always add more along the way—and bring the pan to medium-high heat. Season with salt and cook until the onion is soft and aromatic, 8 to 10 minutes. Add the garlic and cook for another 2 to 3 minutes, stirring frequently.

2 Add the tomatoes and stir to combine. Taste and season with more salt and red pepper if needed. Bring to a boil (BTB) and reduce to a simmer (RTS).

3 Continue cooking until the sauce thickens, 15 to 20 minutes. Remember, it's a dipping sauce, so you want it thick, highly seasoned, and delicious. When it gets there, remove it from

RECIPE CONTINUES

the heat, adjust the seasoning if needed, and . . . get ready to dip!

FOR THE FRITTERS

1 Coat a large sauté pan with olive oil, add the onions, season with salt, and bring the pan to medium-high heat. Cook until the onions are soft and aromatic, 8 to 10 minutes.

2 Add the zucchini, season with salt, and cook for another 7 to 8 minutes, or until the zucchini is soft and just beginning to color on the edges. Remove from the heat and let cool.

3 In a large bowl, combine the flour, Parm, and baking powder. Add the zucchini and onions to the bowl and stir until just combined. Add the milk gradually (you may not need it all) and stir to combine; you want a very thick batter. Don't worry about the lumps.

4 Pour peanut oil into a large saucepan over medium-high heat; the oil should come 1½ to 2 inches up the sides of the pan. While the oil heats, set up your drying situation next to the stove by putting a couple layers of paper towels on a baking sheet. To see if the oil is hot enough, drop a little ball of batter into it. If it sizzles and floats quickly, you're good to go. (If the batter burns or the oil begins to smoke, it's too hot, so reduce the heat.) Drop 1-inch balls of batter into the pan without overcrowding. When the fritters turn nice and brown on all sides, 3 to 4 minutes, remove them with a slotted spoon and drain on the paper towels. Work in batches to finish the rest of the batter. If the fritters begin to color too quickly, lower the heat; if they don't sizzle when they hit the oil, turn it up.

5 When all the fritters are done, serve them with a sprinkey-dink of Parm and the super-yummy spicy tomato sauce.

Holy fritter, Batman!

you can judge the temperature of the oil by what's going on in the pan, but if you feel the need to use a deep-fry thermometer, go ahead!

STIR-FRIED
MARINATED
OLIVES

SERVES: 4 TO 6 · TIME: ABOUT 1½ HOURS, MOSTLY UNATTENDED

Lots of restaurants put a dish of olives on the table, which always seems like a great idea. The bummer is that the olives usually aren't marinated very well and so they're boring. These olives are different: I use all different colors and sizes and add yummy things like big pieces of citrus zest, fennel and coriander seeds, garlic, herbs, and even a little kick of crushed red pepper. The secret is to first warm everything together slowly so the flavors marry; then, once they're marinated, stir-fry them in a SCREAMING hot pan until they blister and frizzle on the outside. (And here's a tip: These olives will hold forever in the fridge and it's just as easy to make a lot as a little—so whip up a big batch, and you'll always have some on hand.) These are SOOOOO delicious you want to eat them right away, but watch out—they're hot stuff!

MISE EN PLACE

2 cups olives, all the same or a mix of sizes and colors

1 tablespoon fennel seeds

1 tablespoon coriander seeds

1 teaspoon crushed red pepper

2 cloves garlic, smashed

Zest of 1 orange, removed in wide strips with a peeler

Zest of 1 lemon, removed in wide strips with a peeler

2 bay leaves

2 sprigs of fresh rosemary

1½ cups extra virgin olive oil

1   In a large saucepan, combine all the ingredients over low heat and warm everything until it bubbles gently, like a Jacuzzi. Continue to cook the olives in their warm oil bath for about 20 minutes; they should be very aromatic. Turn off the heat and let everything cool to room temperature (this will take about an hour). If you want to do this step ahead of time, put the olives in a jar in the fridge until you're ready to fry them—the olive oil will solidify but don't worry; it will melt when reheated.

2   When you're ready to serve the olives, bring a large sauté pan to high heat—you want to get it EXTREMELY hot. Add the cooled olive mixture to the pan, shaking it every few seconds until the olives blister on the outside, then remove from the heat.

3   Put the olives and all the other good stuff in a dish and serve immediately, but remember—inside the hot olives is hot olive oil, so be careful!

Aaahhh-luuuv these!!!

TRUFFLED DEVILED EGGS

SERVES: 8 · TIME: ABOUT 20 MINUTES

I'm from upstate New York and we're big deviled egg lovers. Growing up there were always deviled eggs at parties and picnics, so now, anytime I throw a party I make sure to have them, and if I don't, I hear about it. They're always the first thing to disappear at my parties!

When I was developing my piccolini menu at Café Centro, I wanted to have deviled eggs on the menu but I had to figure out a way to make them with an Italian slant. My friend Christina suggested I put truffles in them, and to this day I kick myself for not thinking of that myself, because trust me, these are some kick-ass eggs!

MISE EN PLACE

12 large eggs
1 cup mayonnaise

1 tablespoon truffle oil
Pinch of cayenne pepper
2 tablespoons finely chopped black truffle peelings

Chopped fresh chives, for garnish

1 Put the eggs in a large pot and add enough water to cover by about 1 inch. Bring the pot to a boil (BTB), cover, then turn off the heat and let sit for 13 minutes EXACTLY!

2 Drain the eggs and run them under cold water until cool; if you're not using them right away, put them in the fridge.

3 Peel the eggs and cut them in half lengthwise; remove the yolks. Put the yolks in a small bowl and mash them with a fork; add the mayonnaise, truffle oil, cayenne, and truffle peelings and whip until very light and fluffy.

4 Use a disposable pastry bag (or just buy zip-top bags, fill them, and cut off one corner—a very low-tech solution but my favorite kind!) to pipe the yolk mixture into the whites (or just spoon it in). Sprinkle with the chives to serve.

Eggs-traordinary!

want to goose up the truffle-y flavor? add a dash more truffle oil. but proceed with caution: It's very easy to over truffle!

FIGS

STUFFED WITH GORGONZOLA & WALNUTS

SERVES: 6 TO 8 · TIME: ABOUT 10 MINUTES

People think fresh figs are elegant—and this preparation definitely is. To be honest, figs are not my favorite fruit, but when I make them this way I really love 'em. They are a quick and easy (Q&E) piccolino. Cut 'em, stuff 'em, and roast 'em until everything melts and gets all toasty—it's SOOOOO easy!

MISE EN PLACE

12 fresh Black Mission, Brown Turkish, or (in a pinch) dried figs

High-quality balsamic vinegar

Kosher salt

8 ounces Gorgonzola Dolce, at room temperature

½ cup walnuts, quartered and toasted (see page 17)

1 Preheat the oven to 350°F.

2 Slice the figs in half lengthwise, place them on a baking sheet, and dig a little hole in the middle with your pinky finger. Drizzle the fig halves with 2 or 3 drops of balsamic vinegar and sprinkle with salt.

3 Fill each fig with Gorgonzola and top with a quarter of a walnut. Bake for 5 minutes or until the cheese is melted and bubbly.

Fig out!

CHICKEN LIVER PÂTÉ
WITH BALSAMIC ONIONS

SERVES: 6 TO 8 · TIME: ABOUT 45 MINUTES

I learned how to make this recipe in Tuscany, and who knew all these funky ingredients put together could taste SOOOOO delightful? Chicken livers? Anchovies? Capers? Believe it or not, all these super-strong personalities come together to make one really delicious pâté—and it's so easy. Top this combo with some onions braised in balsamic vinegar and you've got yourself a super Tuscan!

MISE EN PLACE

1 cup balsamic vinegar

FOR THE ONIONS
Extra virgin olive oil
3 onions, thinly sliced
Kosher salt

FOR THE PÂTÉ
Extra virgin olive oil
2 to 3 anchovy fillets
2 tablespoons capers

2 cloves garlic, smashed
1 pound chicken livers, rinsed
1 cup dry white wine
Kosher salt

1 baguette, cut into ½-inch slices, toasted or grilled

FOR THE ONIONS

1 Coat a large sauté pan with olive oil, add the onions, and season with salt; bring the pan to medium-high heat. Cover and sweat the onions for 15 to 20 minutes, or until soft and beginning to color.

2 Add the balsamic vinegar and cook, uncovered, for another 20 minutes or until it becomes syrupy. Taste and reseason if needed. Remove from the heat and set aside.

FOR THE PÂTÉ

1 Coat a large sauté pan with olive oil and add the anchovies, capers, and garlic. Bring to medium heat and cook, stirring occasionally, until the anchovies dissolve, 3 to 4 minutes.

2 Add the chicken livers, turn the heat to high, and cook for 5 to 6 minutes, stirring occasionally. Add the wine and cook for 4 to 5 more minutes or until the wine has reduced by half; the mix will still be pretty soupy.

3 Transfer the mixture to a food processor and purée until smooth. Season with a little salt and loosen with a little olive oil if needed. Schmear each toast with the pâté and top with the balsamic onions to serve.

Killer! Chopped liver!

If you have leftover balsamic onions, these are yummy on sandwiches or on their own - they add a sweet-sour tang to lots of thangs!

PERONATA

WITH GOAT CHEESE

SERVES: 6 TO 8 · TIME: ABOUT 30 MINUTES

For me, peppers are the gift that keeps on giving. Whenever I eat a roasted pepper it seems to stay with me forever. My sister, who's a dietician, told me it's because they have so little acid in them. Knowing this, I came up with a way to do two cool things—eat peppers without having them stick around all day and make a yummy peperonata—simply by adding a bit of sherry vinegar (a.k.a. acid) to the mix.

The vinegar adds a lovely brightness to this dish, and the pimentón (smoked paprika) gives it a rich smokiness—both of which are unbelievably good with the creaminess of the goat cheese. Of course, you don't have to serve this with goat cheese the way I do; you can make a batch of peperonata just to have in the fridge to throw on a sandwich—like a condiment—or to pull out and serve on bread when someone comes over for a drink. This is one of my personal super-secret flavor weapons!

MISE EN PLACE

Extra virgin olive oil

2 onions, cut into ½-inch dice

Pinch of crushed red pepper

Kosher salt

2 cloves garlic, smashed

1 red and 1 yellow bell pepper, stemmed, seeded, pith removed, and cut into ½-inch diamonds

¼ cup tomato paste

½ teaspoon pimentón (smoked paprika)

2 tablespoons sherry vinegar

1 8- to 10-ounce log of goat cheese, at room temp

Chopped fresh chives, for garnish (optional)

1 baguette, cut into ½-inch slices, toasted or grilled

1 Coat a large sauté pan with olive oil, add the onions and red pepper, season with salt, and bring to medium heat. Cook the onions until soft and aromatic, 8 to 10 minutes, stirring occasionally to make sure they don't brown.

2 Add the garlic and cook for another 2 to 3 minutes; it should start to smell really good!

3 Add the peppers and ¼ cup water; season with salt. Continue cooking until the peppers have softened and the water has evaporated, another 8 to 10 minutes.

4 Add the tomato paste, pimentón, and sherry vinegar and stir to combine; taste for salt (it will probably need more). Cook until the mixture comes together and looks tightened up and slightly thickened, 6 to 7 minutes. Remove from the heat and let cool.

5 I like to squish the goat cheese into a serving bowl and nestle the peperonata in the center rather than spooning it over an entire log—it's more rustic-looking this way. Garnish with chives if you like and serve with baguette slices.

Collect your kudos!

SAUSAGE & PANCETTA
STUFFED
MUSHROOMS

MAKES: APPROXIMATELY 30 · TIME: ABOUT 20 MINUTES

These mushrooms are double-stuffed with pork so even if you think you don't like mushrooms, remember, they're just the vessel for a double dose of porky deliciousness! I make these all the time and here's a tip: Always make a small tester patty out of the stuffing before filling all the caps. Cook the patty and taste it to make sure it's delicious. It may sound like an unnecessary step, but it's one you don't want to skip. There's nothing fun about an underseasoned mushroom!

MISE EN PLACE

Extra virgin olive oil

¼ pound pancetta, cut into ¼-inch dice

2 onions, finely diced

Pinch of crushed red pepper

Kosher salt

2 cloves garlic, smashed and finely chopped

1 pound cremini mushrooms, cleaned, stems removed and finely chopped, caps reserved

1 tablespoon finely chopped fresh rosemary

½ cup dry white wine

½ pound sweet Italian sausage, casings removed

1 large egg

½ cup freshly grated Parmigiano

½ cup bread crumbs

1 Preheat the oven to 375°F.

2 Coat a large sauté pan with olive oil, add the pancetta, and bring to medium-high heat. Cook the pancetta until it starts to brown and crisp on the edges, 6 to 8 minutes. Add the onions and the red pepper and season with salt. Continue cooking until the onions are soft and aromatic, 8 to 10 minutes. Add the garlic and cook for another 2 to 3 minutes, stirring frequently.

3 Stir in the mushroom stems and rosemary and cook until the mushrooms are brown and soft, 5 to 6 minutes. Add the wine and cook until evaporated. Remove from the heat and cool.

4 Meanwhile, in a large bowl combine the sausage, egg, Parm, and bread crumbs; add the mushroom mixture, season, and mix well (if the filling seems a little dry, add ¼ to ½ cup water to moisten things up).

5 Make a 1- to 2-inch tester patty out of the stuffing mixture. In a small sauté pan, heat a bit of oil and cook the patty until it's done. When it's cool enough, taste your tester patty to make sure it's delicious—if it's not, reseason.

6 When your tester tastes fabulous, generously fill each mushroom cap with the stuffing mixture and arrange them on a rimmed baking sheet. Pour ¼ to ⅓ cup water into the pan to keep the mushrooms moist. Bake until the filling is cooked through and brown and crispy on top, 7 to 8 minutes. Transfer to serving platters.

Mmmmm . . . magic mushrooms!

OYSTER MUSHROOM CHIPS

SERVES: 4 · TIME: ABOUT 15 MINUTES

These are one of my favorite things to make: oyster mushrooms tossed with olive oil, salt, and crushed red pepper. They're salty and spicy and they taste like bacon! To me they're kind of like mushroom jerky. Who knew an oyster mushroom could be so delicious?

MISE EN PLACE

1½ pounds oyster mushrooms, stemmed and torn into bite-size pieces

Extra virgin olive oil

Kosher salt

¼ teaspoon crushed red pepper, or to taste

1 Preheat the oven to 375°F.

2 Put the mushrooms in a large bowl and toss with olive oil until lightly coated; season with salt and red pepper. Using two baking sheets, spread the mushrooms in a single layer; you don't want them to overlap.

3 Roast the mushrooms for 10 to 12 minutes, or until brown and "cooked on" or stuck to the baking sheet. Remove from the oven and let cool for 5 minutes. Use a bench scrape to get the mushroom chips off the bottom of the baking sheet. Transfer to a dish and serve.

Mmmmm . . . mushroom chips!

EGGPLANT
CAKES
WITH RICOTTA

SERVES: 4 TO 6 · TIME: ABOUT 1½ HOURS

If you think you don't like eggplant, I bet this recipe will change your mind. And if you do like eggplant, feel free to make these bigger for a yummy eggplant burger!

MISE EN PLACE

Extra virgin olive oil

2 onions, cut into ½-inch dice

Kosher salt

Pinch of crushed red pepper, plus more for topping

2 cloves garlic, smashed and finely chopped

3 plum tomatoes, seeded and diced

1 eggplant, strips of skin removed lengthwise (it should look striped!), cut into 1-inch dice

½ bunch of fresh oregano leaves, finely chopped

½ cup freshly grated Parmigiano

½ cup bread crumbs, plus more for coating

1 cup ricotta cheese

1 Preheat the oven to 400°F.

2 Coat a large sauté pan with olive oil and bring to medium heat. Add the onions, season with salt and red pepper, and cook until soft and very aromatic, 8 to 10 minutes. Add the garlic and cook for 2 to 3 more minutes, stirring frequently.

3 Toss in the tomatoes and eggplant and sprinkle with more salt. Cook for 30 minutes, or until the mixture is dry and mushy (you WANT it mushy!), stirring frequently to keep it from burning. Let the mixture cool until you can handle it, about 20 minutes.

4 Toss in the oregano, Parmigiano, and bread crumbs and stir to combine; taste and adjust the seasoning if needed.

5 Put some bread crumbs in a small bowl. Using a tablespoon, scoop out balls of the eggplant mixture and roll them in the bread crumbs. When the balls are well coated, gently flatten them and put them on a baking sheet.

6 Drizzle the "cakes" with olive oil and bake for 10 to 12 minutes or until golden and crispy. Top each cake with a dollop of ricotta and a couple flakes of crushed red pepper, and serve.

Betcha love eggplant now!

BREADSTICK "BROOMS"

Who doesn't love a breadstick? And a breadstick wrapped up with yummy stuff is even better. My recipe for homemade grissini (skinny little breadsticks) is really good, but as I always say, pick your battles. If you don't feel like making them, go ahead and buy some packaged ones—I promise this will still be a crowd pleaser!

MISE EN PLACE

1 cup all-purpose flour, plus more as needed

1 teaspoon baking powder

½ teaspoon baking soda

1 teaspoon sugar

1½ teaspoons kosher salt

¼ teaspoon cayenne pepper

2 tablespoons finely chopped fresh rosemary

½ cup whole milk

1 teaspoon lemon juice

1 tablespoon extra virgin olive oil

½ pound prosciutto, thinly sliced

½ pound baby arugula

1 Preheat the oven to 350°F. and line a baking sheet with parchment paper.

2 Put the flour, baking powder, baking soda, sugar, salt, cayenne, and rosemary in a large bowl and whisk to combine. Make a well in the center of the dry ingredients and add the milk, lemon juice, and olive oil; using a fork, gently stir the wet ingredients into the dry until a dough forms.

3 Put the dough on a well-floured work surface, shape it into a ball, and, using the heels of your hands, knead it for about a minute. If the dough sticks, sprinkle it with a bit of flour.

4 Roll the dough in a log and cut it into about twenty-four 1-inch pieces. Using both hands, roll each piece of dough into a 7-inch rope; don't worry if they're not all exactly the same. Put them on the parchment-lined baking sheet.

5 Bake the breadsticks until golden and crispy, 20 to 25 minutes. Remove them from the oven and let the little lovelies cool.

6 Cut the prosciutto slices in half widthwise and lay a few arugula leaves in a bunch on one end of each slice. Put the end of a breadstick on the arugula and roll up the arugula and prosciutto, pressing lightly to secure—the finished product should look like a wacky little broom! Repeat with all the breadsticks.

Watch out—these will clean up!

When rolling out the Grissini, don't worry if the ropes aren't perfectly shaped; you want them a bit knobby in places - it's more 'rustic!

POLPETTINI
(YUMMY LITTLE MEATBALLS)

MAKES: APPROXIMATELY 80 TO 100 · TIME: ABOUT 25 MINUTES

Polpettini are delightful little Tuscan meatballs. I love them bite-size, but you can also take this mix and make one big log called a *polpettone*—either way, it's delicious! And here's a tip: For cute and easy serving, cut 1-inch rosemary sprigs to use as toothpicks.

MISE EN PLACE

Extra virgin olive oil

3 onions, cut into ¼-inch dice

Kosher salt

3 cloves garlic, smashed and finely chopped

½ pound ground beef

½ pound ground veal

½ pound ground pork

3 tablespoons finely chopped fresh rosemary

¾ cup freshly grated Parmigiano

½ cup bread crumbs

3 large eggs

2 cups chicken stock (see page 85)

1 Coat a large sauté pan with olive oil and bring to medium heat. Add the onions, season with salt, and cook until soft and very aromatic, 8 to 10 minutes. Add the garlic and cook for 2 to 3 more minutes. Remove from the heat and cool.

2 Transfer the onions to a large bowl and add the beef, veal, pork, rosemary, Parmigiano, ¼ cup water, bread crumbs, and eggs; season generously with salt. Use your hands to combine everything well—it's squishy and fun! The mixture should be pretty loosey-goosey, so add 1 to 2 tablespoons more water if needed.

3 Before cooking all the polpettini, make a 1- to 2-inch tester patty. In a small sauté pan, heat a bit of oil and cook the patty; when it's cool enough, taste it to make sure it's delicious—if it's not, reseason. When the tester tastes fabulous, roll the mixture into 1-inch balls.

4 Coat a large sauté pan with olive oil and bring it to high heat. Working in batches so you don't overcrowd the pan, cook the polpettini until brown on all sides, then add ½ cup of the chicken stock and cook until the stock has reduced by half, 2 to 3 minutes. Remove the polpettini and reserve in a warm spot. Repeat this process until all the polpettini are cooked. Stick them with rosemary toothpicks to serve.

Have a ball!

remember, a tester patty is a super-important step, so don't skip it!

HARD POLENTA CAKES

WITH TALEGGIO & CHERRY TOMATOES

SERVES: 8 · TIME: ABOUT 2 HOURS, MOSTLY UNATTENDED

I love to make these for company because the polenta can be made WAY in advance. And you can top the cakes with almost anything—I like to use a nice stinky cheese, but after that really anything goes. Tomatoes give you a nice burst of sweetness, but dried fruit is fun, some fresh herbs, whatever you want! No matter how you top them, these corn cakes are little bites of melty, cheesy deliciousness.

MISE EN PLACE

1 cup whole milk, plus more as needed

1 bay leaf

Pinch of cayenne pepper

Kosher salt

¾ cup polenta

½ cup mascarpone

½ cup freshly grated Parmigiano

½ pound Taleggio, rind removed, cut into ½-inch cubes

1 pint cherry tomatoes, cut in half lengthwise

Extra virgin olive oil

Coarse sea salt for finishing

1 bunch of fresh chives, finely chopped

1 Combine the milk, 2 cups water, bay leaf, and cayenne in a medium saucepan. Bring to a boil (BTB) and season generously with kosher salt. You want to take the seasoning to the edge of too salty in this case; to do this you MUST taste as you go! Polenta acts like a "salt eraser," and if you don't salt abundantly in this early step, you'll never recover.

2 When the liquid is boiling, gradually sprinkle in the polenta, whisking constantly. Once the polenta is combined, IMMEDIATELY switch to a wooden spoon and stir frequently until the polenta thickens; this will take 30 to 35 minutes. Taste the polenta to see if it's cooked through; if it still feels mealy and grainy, add some more milk or water and continue to cook for another 10 minutes. Repeat this process as needed until the polenta feels smooth on your tongue. Remove the bay leaf and stir in the mascarpone and Parmigiano; reserve.

3 Line a 7-inch square pan with plastic wrap. Pour the polenta mixture into the prepared pan and cover with plastic, pressing down so the

plastic sits on the surface of the polenta. Chill until set, at least 45 minutes. (All of this can totally be done ahead of time—like yesterday!)

4   Preheat the oven to 400°F.

5   When the polenta is set, cut it into 1-inch squares. Put the squares on a baking sheet and top each with a piece of Taleggio.

6   Put the cherry tomatoes on a separate baking sheet and toss them with olive oil. Bake both the polenta squares and the tomatoes for 10 minutes. The tomatoes should be hot, starting to relax, and getting a little squishy, and the Taleggio should be nicely melted.

7   Put the polenta cakes on a serving dish, top each square with a cherry tomato half, and garnish each with a little sprinkey-dink of coarse sea salt and chives.

What a corn cake!!!

polenta starts to bubble like hot lava fields and if it gets on you it will stick and burn—so watch out!

ANNE ALTERNATE   If you're not a stinky-cheese person, use whatever cheese you want—remember, you're the chef of your own kitchen!

PARMIGIANO-CRUSTED CAULIFLOWER

WITH GARLIC DIPPER

SERVES: 6 TO 8 · TIME: ABOUT 45 MINUTES

Cauliflower is one of my favorite vegetables. I love to jack it up with some bread crumbs and Parm and deep-fry it till it's nice and brown. These are little bites of crunchy, cheesy, salty, heavenly loveliness. Add some garlicky goodness in the form of a dipping sauce and you have a showstopper!

MISE EN PLACE

FOR THE CAULIFLOWER

Kosher salt

1 head of cauliflower, cut into bite-size florets

2 cups peanut or other neutral-flavored oil

1 cup all-purpose flour

2 large eggs, beaten with 2 tablespoons water

1 cup bread crumbs

1 cup freshly grated Parmigiano

FOR THE GARLIC DIPPER

2 cups day-old or stale rustic Italian bread, crusts removed and cubed

2 tablespoons red wine vinegar, or to taste

2 cloves garlic, smashed

½ cup extra virgin olive oil

Kosher salt

FOR THE CAULIFLOWER

1 Bring a large pot of well-salted water to a boil, set up a large bowl of well-salted ice water, and line a baking sheet with paper towels. Toss the cauliflower florets into the boiling water. When the water returns to a boil, cook the cauliflower for 2 more minutes, then drain and immediately plunge into the ice water. When the cauliflower has cooled, drain it and lay it out to dry on the prepared baking sheet. (While you wait, you can get your dipper going—now that's what I call multitasking!)

2 Pour the peanut oil into a large saucepan over medium-high heat; the oil should come 1½ to 2 inches up the sides of the pan. To see if it's hot enough, drop some flour into it. If the flour sizzles and floats quickly, you're good to go. If the flour burns or the oil begins to smoke, it's too hot, so reduce the heat.

3 While the oil heats, set up your standard breading procedure (see opposite): one bowl of flour, one bowl with the egg-water mixture, and one with the bread crumbs and grated Parm.

STANDARD BREADING PROCEDURE
(a.k.a. The Way to Coat Stuff for Deep-Frying)

The point of the standard breading procedure is to coat something—anything, really—in bread crumbs so when it's fried, it comes out with a nice even, crispy coating. The key ingredients here are flour, egg wash, and bread crumbs, but there are two pieces of essential equipment that are often forgotten—the wet hand and the dry hand. In between these two essentials is the continental divide, and never the two shall cross.

Start by using your dry hand to coat whatever ingredient you plan to fry in flour and shake off the excess. Then, still using your dry hand, pick up the ingredient and drop it into the egg wash without letting your dry hand get wet. Then, using your wet hand, pick up your ingredient and drop it into the bread crumbs. Switch back to your dry hand to pack on the bread crumbs for a firm, even coating. By following this simple dry-wet-dry-hand approach, your ingredients will be properly breaded AND there will be no clumpage on the ends of your fingers. Ta-da!

Then set up your drying situation next to the stove by putting a couple layers of paper towels on a baking sheet. When the oil is hot, dredge the cauliflower in the flour and shake off the excess, then run it through the egg mixture, and finally through the bread crumb–Parm mixture. Repeat this process with all the cauliflower.

4   Working in batches so you don't overcrowd the pan, fry the cauliflower until brown and crispy, 3 to 5 minutes; then transfer to the paper towels, sprinkle with salt, and serve hot, hot, hot with the garlic dipper.

FOR THE DIPPER

In a medium bowl, toss the bread with enough water to really moisten it up; you want it almost soggy. Then squeeze out the excess water and put the bread, vinegar, and garlic in a food processor and purée, purée, purée—it should be really smooth! While the machine is still running, drizzle in the olive oil until combined. Season with salt and more vinegar if you like—I like a very bright, acidic dipping sauce. Put the dipper in a dish and serve it along with the cauliflower.

Mmmmm . . . salty, crispy, crunchy cauliflower and garlicky gooooodness!

CIPOLLINE TEMPURA
WITH AÏOLI

SERVES: 6 TO 8 · TIME: ABOUT 30 MINUTES

Cipolline are flat, sweet Italian onions that look like little flying saucers. I love these guys because they're like onion rings with no holes. Perfectly fried baby onions and garlic mayonnaise to dip them in—they're out of this world!

MISE EN PLACE

FOR THE CIPOLLINE TEMPURA
Kosher salt
1 pound small cipolline onions
1 cup cake or rice flour
1 tablespoon baking powder

½ to ¾ cup ice-cold sparkling water
2 cups peanut or other neutral-flavored oil

FOR THE AÏOLI
2 egg yolks
3 tablespoons red wine vinegar

2 cloves garlic, smashed
Pinch of crushed red pepper, or to taste
Peanut or other neutral-flavored oil
Kosher salt

FOR THE TEMPURA

1 Bring a medium pot of well-salted water to a boil. Toss in the cipolline and cook for 5 to 7 minutes or until tender. Drain and let cool. (While these are cooling, I suggest you save time and whip up your aïoli. BTW, this is multitasking!)

2 When the onions are cool enough to handle, use a paring knife to peel off the outer skin and trim the hairy root end; reserve.

3 To make the tempura batter, combine the flour, baking powder, and ½ teaspoon salt in a large bowl. Add the cold (seriously—ice-cold!) sparkling water and mix until a loose batter forms; don't worry about the lumps.

4 When you're ready to cook, pour the peanut oil into a large saucepan over medium-high heat; the oil should come 1½ to 2 inches up the sides of the pan. To see if it's hot enough, drop a couple of little batter balls into it. If they sizzle and float quickly, you're good to go. If the batter burns or the oil begins to smoke, it's too hot, so reduce the heat.

5 While the oil heats, set up your drying situation next to the stove by putting a couple layers of paper towels on a baking sheet. Dip and coat each of the onions in the tempura batter, then add them one at a time to the oil. Work in batches—you don't want to overcrowd the pan—and fry them until the batter is crisp but still pale and golden. Remove the onions from the oil and salt these puppies immediately.

In the bowl of a food processor, combine the egg yolks, vinegar, garlic, and red pepper and process until combined. Then, with the machine running, begin to add the oil a drop at a time—you want to do this slowly in the beginning until the mixture begins to thicken and look homogeneous. Once this happens, add the remaining oil in a thin stream until it is all combined; taste and season with salt. Serve the garlicky mayonnaise with the crispy sweet onions.

Take THAT, onion rings!

WHITE BEAN PURÉE
WITH PROSCIUTTO

SERVES: 6 TO 8 · TIME: ABOUT 2 HOURS, MOSTLY UNATTENDED

This is not your ordinary bean dip. A lovely combo of beans, veggies, rosemary, and prosciutto makes this a simple but sophisticated twist on an old standby—and, while I recommend cooking your own beans, popping open a can instead is totally acceptable in a pinch.

MISE EN PLACE

½ pound cannellini beans, soaked overnight (see opposite)

3 onions, 1 peeled and cut in half, 2 cut into ¼-inch dice

1 celery rib, trimmed

1 carrot

2 cloves garlic, smashed

2 bay leaves

1 thyme bundle, tied with butcher's twine

Kosher salt

Extra virgin olive oil

Pinch of crushed red pepper

½ cup prosciutto scraps, finely diced

2 tablespoons finely chopped fresh rosemary

ANNE ALERT!

This recipe is best when you cook your own beans, so plan ahead.

1 Put the beans, onion halves, celery, carrot, garlic, bay leaves, and thyme in a large pot and cover with water—it should come at least 2 inches above the level of the beans. Bring to a boil (BTB) and reduce to a simmer (RTS); cook until the beans are tender when you taste them, an hour or more. To be sure they're done, do the 5-Bean Test (opposite).

2 When the beans are cooked through, turn off the heat, season the water generously with salt, and let sit for 20 minutes. Remove the onion halves, celery, carrot, garlic, bay leaves, and thyme and strain the beans, reserving about a cup of liquid to loosen the purée later if needed.

3 Coat a large sauté pan generously with olive oil, add the diced onion and red pepper, and bring to medium heat; season with salt and cook until the onions are soft and aromatic, 8 to 10 minutes. Add the prosciutto and rosemary and sauté for 3 to 4 more minutes, or until the meat just begins to color. Add the beans and some of the reserved bean cooking liquid if the mixture seems dry. Sauté for 2 or 3 minutes or until the beans are just warm.

BEANS, BEANS, THE MUSICAL FRUIT

Bean cooking SHOULD go like this: Toss the beans in a bowl of water and let them sit overnight. The next morning, put the beans in a pot with an onion cut in half, a whole rib of celery, a whole carrot, a couple of garlic cloves, some bay leaves, and a thyme bundle (and yes, you do want to leave all these veggies whole—it makes them much easier to remove later on). Cover everything with about 2 inches of water and BTB, RTS—bring to a boil, reduce to a simmer.

Now, if you didn't remember to soak your beans yesterday, you can do the quick-cook method (which really isn't that quick). Toss the beans and all the veggies together in a pot, bring to a boil (BTB), turn off the heat, and let it cool back down. This does the same thing as soaking your beans overnight. By the way, this works for all beans except for chickpeas—I don't know why, they're stubborn.

The only way to know for sure if your beans are done is to taste them, because different beans take different amounts of time to cook. To tell if beans are done, perform the 5-Bean Test: Taste at least five beans—if any of them are hard, then they're not all done! When the beans are tender, turn off the heat, season generously with salt, remove the veg, and strain the beans from the bean cooking liquid. Voilà! Perfectly cooked and perfectly seasoned beans . . . every time.

4 Transfer everything to a food processor and purée until smooth, adding a bit of olive oil or reserved cooking liquid to loosen the purée if necessary. Taste, adding more salt if needed. Serve on bread or wherever bean dip is needed.

BEAN there, done that!

don't use your big-money prosciutto here. ask your butcher to sell you the ends, which are usually the leftover bits they can't sell.

GRILLED
CORN, BACON & CHILI CROSTINI

SERVES: 4 TO 6 · TIME: ABOUT 30 MINUTES

I always say everything tastes better with bacon. And when fresh corn is at its peak and just screaming to be eaten, this recipe is unbeatable (it also reminds me of summer as a kid because it was always my job to shuck the corn). It's the perfect combination of smoky, sweet, spicy, and bright—what more could you ask for, except maybe MORE!

MISE EN PLACE

2 ears of corn, shucked
Extra virgin olive oil
Kosher salt

4 strips of bacon, julienned
2 Fresno chilies, cut into thin rounds, seeding optional
3 to 4 tablespoons red wine vinegar

4 scallions, white and green parts, sliced thinly on the bias
1 baguette, cut into ½-inch slices on the bias
1 clove garlic

1 Preheat a grill.

2 Lightly brush the corn with olive oil and sprinkle with salt. Put the corn on the grill and cook, turning every 2 or 3 minutes, until the kernels are charred and soft. Remove and let cool. Once you can handle it, stand the corn upright in a wide bowl and carefully run a knife down each ear lengthwise to cut the kernels off the cob; reserve.

3 Coat a sauté pan with olive oil, add the bacon, and bring to medium heat. When the bacon is brown and crispy, 8 to 10 minutes, add the chili peppers and sauté for 2 to 3 minutes more. Add the corn and toss to combine. Season with salt, stir in the vinegar, and taste—it should be really good by now. Toss in the scallions, remove from heat, and reserve.

4 Toast the baguette slices on the grill; when lightly charred on both sides, 3 to 4 minutes total, remove them and rub each slice with the whole garlic clove. Drizzle with olive oil and top with the corn-bacon mixture.

This is super-corny!

TOMATO-BASIL BRUSCHETTA

This is a classic that everyone should know how to do well. The trick here has nothing to do with cooking and everything to do with using only seasonal ingredients. When summer tomatoes are pristine and basil is at its peak, that's when you want to whip this baby up. By the way, it's pronounced "broo-SKET-ta"—NOT "broo-SHETT-ta."

MISE EN PLACE

4 large tomatoes, seeded and cut into ¼-inch dice

6 to 8 fresh basil leaves, cut into a chiffonade (see below)

2 tablespoons red wine vinegar, or to taste

Kosher salt

2 cloves garlic, smashed and finely chopped, plus 1 whole clove

¼ cup big fat finishing oil

1 baguette, cut into ½-inch slices on the bias

1 Preheat a grill.

2 Combine the tomatoes, basil, vinegar, salt, smashed garlic, and big fat finishing oil in a large bowl, toss well, and reserve.

3 Toast the baguette slices on the grill; when lightly charred on both sides, 3 to 4 minutes total, remove them and rub each slice with the whole garlic clove. Top with the lovely tomato-basil mixture.

This is summer on toast!

A chiffonade is a thin ribbon cut used for fresh basil, mint, and other fragile leaves that can bruise very easily, turn black, and look gross. To chiffonade, you can either cut the herbs with kitchen shears or roll up the herbs and run through them with a very sharp knife. Either way, you don't want to crash your knife (especially a dull one!) down on top of the leaves or they'll certainly turn black. Ick.

BAKED RICOTTA
WITH ROSEMARY & LEMON

SERVES: 4 TO 6 · TIME: ABOUT 20 MINUTES

This is another super-cinchy piccolini that packs a big wow factor. Start with high-quality ricotta, mix it up with lots of other yummy stuff, put it in a cute dish, and bake until it's all warm and melty. Serve this cheesy pot of deliciousness with lots of warm bread, and I guarantee people will call you a rock star!

MISE EN PLACE

2 cups ricotta cheese

3 sprigs of fresh rosemary, leaves finely chopped

Grated zest of 1 lemon

3 tablespoons extra virgin olive oil

Pinch of crushed red pepper

Kosher salt

Big fat finishing oil

1 loaf of rustic Italian bread, cut into 1-inch slices

1 Preheat the oven to 375°F.

2 Combine the ricotta, rosemary, zest, olive oil, red pepper, and salt in a large bowl and mix well. Taste to make sure it's delicious and reseason as needed.

3 Transfer the mixture to an ovenproof dish and bake for 12 to 15 minutes or until heated through. Remove from the oven, drizzle with a little bit of big fat finishing oil, and serve immediately with the bread.

Hot and cheeeeesy!

FIRSTS

{ the introduction }

· ·

I LOOOOVE appetizers. Nothing's easier than walking into a restaurant, getting a glass of wine, and saying, "Let's grab some apps!" They're usually crispy and crunchy, gooey and cheesy, or bright and refreshing. They give you just enough of a taste to really appreciate how all the flavors work together, and the really good appetizers leave you wanting more.

· ·

I DISCOVERED THE BEAUTY AND CREATIVITY OF THE FIRST COURSE when I was studying in Italy. I was going to school in Piedmont, way up in the northwest, the land of white truffles, Barolo, and Barbaresco. But Piedmont is also the land of antipasti—the Italian word for appetizer. Needless to say, it was quite an education.

When I'd go to a restaurant, the waiter would ask how many antipasti we wanted, three or four? I was in heaven! Antipasti are the beginning of the journey—they're the first flavors you experience, they excite your taste buds, but they don't fill you up; they're just a few small bites to get your juices going before you move on to what's next. Great appetizers are sometimes the most satisfying part of the meal. They're small, there's a huge variety, and they're sexy!

As a chef I find that appetizers also offer a ton of room for creativity. In fact, when I go out to dinner I often order just two appetizers—one to start and one for my main—because they're frequently the most interesting dishes on the menu. I think you'll find these recipes will help you on your way to loving the first course as much as I do.

Calamari Noodles with Fingerling Potatoes
& Black Olives

Garlic Steamed Mussels with Pimentón Aïoli

Ricotta-Stuffed Zucchini Blossoms with Panzanella
(a.k.a. Yummy Bread Salad)

Grilled Pizzetta with Stracchino, Sausage,
Arugula, & Chili Oil

Escarole Salad with Walnuts, Pecorino & Pickled Onions

Grilled Porcini with Poached Egg & Parmigiano

Heirloom Tomato Salad with Warm Goat Cheese

Grilled Shrimp with Chickpea Fries,
Zucchini & Pine Nut Salad

Grilled Sea Scallops with a Watermelon
Three-Way & Dandelion Greens

Grilled Soft-Shell Crabs with Asparagus,
Arugula & Spring Onion Salad with Aïoli

Spiced Chickpea Soup with Crispy, Crunchy Croutons

Oysters on the Half Shell with Prosecco "Sno-Cone"

Pumpkin Soup with Allspice Whipped Cream
& Fried Leeks

Raw Asparagus, Red Onion & Pecorino Salad

Roasted Beet & Many-Herb Salad

My Big Fat Chicken Soup

Parmigiano Flan

Sugar Snap Pea Salad with Crispy Prosciutto & Mint

CALAMARI NOODLES

WITH FINGERLING POTATOES
& BLACK OLIVES

SERVES: 4 · TIME: ABOUT 30 MINUTES

I'm always looking for new things to do with calamari. It's inexpensive, and if you buy it already cleaned—which I HIGHLY recommend—it's super Q&E (quick and easy) to use. This recipe is fun because it takes minimum effort and you get maximum kudos at the dinner table.

MISE EN PLACE

1 pound cleaned calamari, tubes and tentacles (or only tubes, if you prefer)

Extra virgin olive oil

3 or 4 cloves garlic, smashed, plus 1 whole clove

Pinch of crushed red pepper

4 fingerling potatoes, unpeeled and cut into ¼-inch rounds

Kosher salt

1 cup dry white wine

¼ cup kalamata or gaeta olives, slivered

4 thick slices of rustic Italian bread

2 cups baby arugula

2 tablespoons chopped fresh chives, for garnish

1 Cut each calamari tube into ¼-inch strips lengthwise. If using the tentacles, cut into segments.

2 Coat a large sauté pan generously with olive oil. Add the smashed garlic cloves and red pepper and bring to high heat. When the garlic is golden brown and very aromatic, 2 to 3 minutes, remove it from the pan and ditch it—it has fulfilled its garlic destiny!

3 Add the potatoes to the garlic-infused oil and bring to medium-high heat; cook until brown on one side, about 5 minutes, then turn and brown the second side. Remove the potatoes from the pan and reserve.

4 Add the calamari to the pan and toss it in the hot oil. Season with salt and cook for 1 to 2 minutes, or until it turns opaque. Add the wine and the olives and continue to cook until the wine has reduced by about half, 3 to 5 minutes. Taste and adjust the seasoning if needed.

5 While the calamari is cooking, toast or grill the bread until charred on both sides, 3 to 4 minutes total. Rub the bread with the remaining garlic clove and drizzle generously with olive oil.

6   Divide the arugula between four serving bowls. Spoon the reserved potatoes, calamari, and the pan juices over the greens. Cut each piece of bread in half on the bias and lay it on top of the calamari; garnish with chives and serve.

What a noodle!

when it comes to cooking with wine— use something you would feel comfy drinking.

GARLIC STEAMED MUSSELS
WITH PIMENTÓN AÏOLI

SERVES: 4 · TIME: ABOUT 15 MINUTES

Mussels are the unsung heroes of the shellfish world; they're cheap, fast, and satisfying. (I wish more things in life were like this!) My favorite part of making a big pot of mussels is dipping a hunk of crusty bread in the broth. That's why I add this lovely aïoli to the mix right before serving. This sexy sauce drips down into the mussel juice, giving it a spectacular flavor and the illusion that it's a cream sauce. It's super-dunkable!

MISE EN PLACE

FOR THE AÏOLI

2 egg yolks

2 cloves garlic, smashed

3 tablespoons sherry vinegar

1½ tablespoons pimentón (smoked paprika)

Kosher salt

1½ cups peanut or other neutral-flavored oil

FOR THE MUSSELS

Extra virgin olive oil

6 to 8 cloves garlic, smashed

½ teaspoon crushed red pepper

3 pounds mussels, debearded and rinsed

4 or 5 sprigs of fresh oregano, leaves coarsely chopped

3 bay leaves

1 bottle dry white wine

1 baguette, cut into 1-inch slices on the bias

3 scallions, white and green parts, thinly sliced on the bias

FOR THE AÏOLI

Put the egg yolks, garlic, vinegar, pimentón, and a sprinkle of salt in a food processor and purée until the mixture is homogeneous. Then, with the machine running, VERY slowly drizzle in some of the oil until the mixture is thick and smooth. When it starts to look like mayonnaise, the rest of the oil can be added in a thin, slow stream; season with salt. You want relatively thin aïoli here. If it's too thick, add a few drops of water to thin it; or on the flip side, if it's too thin, add more oil. TASTE for seasoning, adjust if needed, and refrigerate until ready to use.

FOR THE MUSSELS

1 Coat the bottom of a large pot (big enough to hold all the mussels) with olive oil. Add the garlic and red pepper and bring to medium-high heat; cook until the garlic is golden and very aromatic, 4 to 5 minutes.

2 Add the mussels, oregano, and bay leaves and stir to coat with the oil; add the wine and cover the pot. Steam the mussels for 5 to 6 minutes; if not all the shells are open, continue to cook them all a little longer. While the mussels are steaming, grill the bread.

3 Serve the mussels in bowls with lots of juice from the pot (as much as you like!). Generously drizzle each bowl with the aïoli, garnish with the scallions, and serve the toasted bread alongside.

Holy aïoli!

when it comes to cooking shellfish, the ones that don't open are the freshest — continue to cook them until they give it up!

When you buy mussels, or any shellfish for that matter, make sure you buy them in mesh bags—remember, these guys are alive and they need to breathe! They also need to stay cold, so don't be afraid to ask your fishmonger for a bag of ice to toss in your shopping bag. Scrub the mussels well and refrigerate them until you're ready to cook (but do not put them in a bowl of water!). If any shells are cracked or broken, toss them. The rule is: When in doubt, throw 'em out.

RICOTTA-STUFFED
ZUCCHINI
BLOSSOMS
WITH PANZANELLA
(A.K.A. YUMMY BREAD SALAD)

SERVES: 4 · TIME: ABOUT 1½ HOURS, MOSTLY UNATTENDED

My mom is a florist so I love flowers—especially big orange ones like zucchini blossoms! I make zucchini blossoms stuffed full of creamy ricotta cheese and then fry them until they're golden and crispy. In my opinion, zucchini blossoms are nature's perfect little packages. What's better than a crispy, crunchy, cheesy flower? A crispy, crunchy, cheesy flower on a bread salad—a gorgeous mix of perfectly ripe tomatoes, basil, cucumber, red onion, and bread, which softens when it absorbs all the veggies' wonderful juices.

MISE EN PLACE

FOR THE PANZANELLA

1¼ cups red wine vinegar

1 tablespoon kosher salt

1½ teaspoons sugar

2 shots of Tabasco or other hot sauce

1 clove garlic, smashed

½ small red onion, thinly sliced

½ Kirby cucumber, sliced into ⅛-inch rounds

6 1-inch slices stale Italian bread, crusts removed, and cut into 1-inch cubes

1 pint cherry tomatoes, cut in half

6 fresh basil leaves, cut into a chiffonade (see page 58)

2 to 3 tablespoons big fat finishing oil

FOR THE BLOSSOMS

8 zucchini blossoms

1½ cups ricotta cheese, goat cheese, mozzarella, or any other good melting cheese

½ cup freshly grated Parmigiano

1 bunch of fresh Italian parsley, leaves finely chopped

Kosher salt

Peanut or other neutral-flavored oil

1½ cups all-purpose flour

¾ to 1 cup dry white wine

FOR THE PANZANELLA

1 Combine the vinegar, 1 cup water, the salt, sugar, Tabasco, and garlic in a large jar or other container with a tight-fitting lid and shake, shake, shake to combine. Add the onion and cucumber, shake again, and let sit for at least 1 hour. (You're making pickles here, and this step can totally be done ahead of time—like yesterday!)

2 Put the bread in a large bowl with ½ to 1 cup of water to soften. Squeeze and knead the bread with your hands, then let it sit for 30 minutes.

3 Squeeze out any excess water from the bread, put the bread back in the bowl, and crumble it through your fingers. Toss in the tomatoes, add the pickled onion and cucumber (strain these out and reserve the liquid), and stir to combine. Add the basil and some finishing oil; taste it to make sure it's delicious. Sprinkle in a few drops of the pickling liquid or a bit more oil if needed; reserve.

FOR THE BLOSSOMS

1 Wiggle your finger into the blossom down to the base, where the flower meets the stem, and carefully break off and remove the stamen (be gentle—you don't want to rip through the blossom while doing this). Repeat with all the blossoms.

2 In a medium bowl, combine the ricotta, Parmigiano, and parsley and season with salt— taste and reseason if needed. Put the ricotta mix into a pastry bag, carefully insert the tip of the bag into the flower, and fill; then gently close your hand around the flower to secure it. Place the stuffed blossom on a baking sheet and repeat with the remaining flowers.

3 Pour peanut oil into a large saucepan over medium-high heat; the oil should come 1½ to 2 inches up the sides of the pan. While the oil heats, set up your drying situation next to the stove by putting a couple layers of paper towels on a baking sheet. To see if the oil is hot enough, drop a bit of flour into it. If it sizzles, you're good to go. If the oil begins to smoke, it's too hot, so reduce the heat.

4 Combine the flour and wine in a large bowl to make a very loose batter. Start with ¾ cup of wine and add more if needed.

5 Working in batches, dip each blossom in the batter to coat it and then gently put each blossom in the oil, being careful not to over-crowd the pan. Let the blossoms cook for 1 to 2 minutes, then turn them over; the blossoms are done when they're still light in color but nice and crispy on the outside. Remove the flowers from the oil with a slotted spoon or fish spatula, put them on the paper towels, and immediately sprinkle with salt.

6 Divide the reserved panzanella between serving plates and top each with two crispy blossoms.

Flower power!

GRILLED
PIZZETTA

WITH STRACCHINO, SAUSAGE, ARUGULA & CHILI OIL

MAKES: 6 · TIME: ABOUT 1½ HOURS, MOSTLY UNATTENDED

I love the charred flavor of grilled pizza. You can top it with anything, of course, but this version is one of my favorites. It's crispy and crunchy, kind of like a grilled cracker. Whenever I eat pizza I always give it a sprinkey-dink of crushed red pepper—it's just better with a little kick! That's why I make this infused oil for my pizzetta. It's an amazing way to get a big flavor bump, and while I love this chili oil on pizza, it's great on lots and lots of things.

MISE EN PLACE

FOR THE CHILI OIL

5 to 6 Fresno chili peppers, roughly chopped

1½ cups extra virgin olive oil

FOR THE DOUGH

1½ teaspoons active dry yeast

½ teaspoon sugar

1½ cups all-purpose flour, plus more as needed

½ teaspoon kosher salt

2 tablespoons extra virgin olive oil, plus more for the bowl and grill

FOR THE PIZZA TOPPING

Extra virgin olive oil

½ pound sweet Italian sausage, casings removed

1 pound stracchino or other mild, creamy cheese, such as ricotta, Taleggio, or Fontina, at room temperature

1 bunch of arugula, trimmed

FOR THE CHILI OIL

Bring the chilies and oil to a simmer in a small saucepan; remove from the heat and let the peppers steep in the oil for at least an hour or until the dough has risen and you're ready to make the pizzas. This can be done WAY in advance.

FOR THE DOUGH

1 While the oil steeps (look at you—multitasking!), combine the yeast, sugar, and ½ cup warm (NOT HOT!) water in a small bowl. Stir to combine and let sit for 10 to 15 minutes until foamy and yeasty-smelling.

2 Combine the flour and salt in a large mixing bowl; make a well in the center of the flour and add the olive oil and the yeast mixture. Using a fork, stir until the flour and liquids are well combined. Turn the dough out onto a well-floured, clean work surface and knead until smooth and elastic, 6 to 7 minutes. Lightly coat the mixing bowl with olive oil, return the dough to the bowl, cover with plastic wrap, and let rise in a warm place until the dough has doubled in size, about 1 hour.

RECIPE CONTINUES

When you're making any kind of yeast dough, be sure the water you use is warm—if the water is too hot it will kill the yeast; if it is too cold, the yeast won't activate. A good way to be sure the water is the correct temperature is to run it over your fingers—if it feels nice and warm, it's fine.

3 When the dough is ready, portion it into six golf-ball-size pieces. Dust a work surface with flour and roll each piece of dough into a rectangle (or whatever shape you like; I like irregular shapes). If you're not using the dough right away, wrap each ball individually in plastic and refrigerate until ready to use.

FOR THE TOPPING AND PIZZA ASSEMBLY

1 Preheat the oven to 425°F. and preheat the grill.

2 Coat a large sauté pan with oil, add the sausage, and bring to medium heat. Cook the sausage until brown, 10 to 15 minutes. Remove with a slotted spoon and reserve.

3 Brush the grill with oil and arrange each piece of dough on the grill; you might need to work in batches here. Grill until the dough is stiff and crisp and has lovely grill marks on it, then flip and repeat on the second side, moving occasionally so the bottom doesn't burn.

4 Put the pizzas on baking sheets, schmear each with some stracchino, top with sausage, and put as many pizzas as will comfortably fit in the oven; bake until the cheese has melted, 5 to 7 minutes. Again, you may have to work in batches. Remove the pizzas from the oven, top with arugula, and drizzle with the deliciously spicy chili oil!

Mamma mia, whatta pizza!

i like fresno peppers because they're medium hot, but you can use what you like - if you prefer a hotter or milder chili, knock yourself out!

ESCAROLE SALAD

WITH WALNUTS, PECORINO & PICKLED ONIONS

SERVES: 4 · TIME: ABOUT 1¼ HOURS, MOSTLY UNATTENDED

Escarole is one of those greens I LOOOOOVE to use in a salad. It has a firm texture and an exciting flavor; to me it's a sleeper hit. Whether you cook it or dress it with a nice bright vinaigrette, escarole stands up to whatever you dish out—it's a green with a strong personality. Add a big ol' acid punch with these onions, and this is what I call a party in your mouth.

MISE EN PLACE

FOR THE PICKLED ONIONS

½ cup red wine vinegar

2 tablespoons kosher salt

1 tablespoon sugar

2 or 3 really good shots of Tabasco or other hot sauce

1 red onion, sliced into very thin rings

FOR THE ESCAROLE SALAD

½ cup freshly grated Pecorino

½ cup walnuts, toasted (see page 17)

1 bunch of fresh chives

1 head of escarole, cut into bite-size pieces

Big fat finishing oil

Kosher salt

FOR THE PICKLED ONIONS

Combine the vinegar with ½ cup cold water in a small bowl. Add the salt, sugar, and Tabasco and stir to combine; add the onion and let sit for at least 1 hour.

FOR THE ESCAROLE SALAD

Put the Pecorino, walnuts, and chives in a food processor and pulse until coarsely chopped. In a large bowl, toss the escarole with the walnut mixture and some of the pickled red onions. Dress with a bit of the pickling liquid and finishing oil. Season with salt.

Take a bite and take a bow!

GRILLED
PORCINI
WITH POACHED EGG & PARMIGIANO

SERVES: 4 · TIME: ABOUT 20 MINUTES

I am a huge fan of eggs—and I especially LOOOOOVE them when they're served at a meal other than breakfast (though I love them for breakfast too!). There's something elegant about putting an egg on a salad—and this particular salad combines the earthy meatiness of porcini mushrooms and the runny yolk of an egg, a combo that I think makes this a super-sexy appetizer or a lovely lunch.

MISE EN PLACE

1 pound porcini mushrooms, trimmed, cleaned, and cut in half lengthwise

Extra virgin olive oil

Kosher salt

Crushed red pepper, to taste

4 slices rustic Italian bread, cut in half on the bias

1 clove garlic

Big fat finishing oil

3 tablespoons white vinegar

4 large eggs

2 cups baby arugula

Juice and zest of 1 lemon

¼ cup freshly grated Parmigiano

1 Preheat the grill.

2 In a large bowl, toss the mushrooms with olive oil until lightly coated, then give them a sprinkle of salt and red pepper. Put the mushrooms flat side down on the grill and cook until they start to soften, 4 to 5 minutes. Rotate the mushrooms 90 degrees and grill for another 3 to 4 minutes, then turn them over and grill for 2 to 3 minutes more. The mushrooms should be beautifully marked, soft, and pliable. Remove from the grill and reserve in a warm spot.

3 Grill each slice of bread until lightly charred on both sides, 3 to 4 minutes total. Rub each slice with the garlic clove and drizzle with the big fat finishing oil.

4 While grilling the mushrooms and bread, fill a medium saucepan two-thirds of the way with water; add the vinegar and bring to a boil. Reduce the heat until no bubbles break the surface of the water; the idea is to create an egg Jacuzzi, a very gentle cooking method.

RECIPE CONTINUES

POACHING: GET OVER IT

Poaching is a way to cook eggs in water *outside* of the shell. The key here is acidulated water—a very big term for water that has acid added to it. Usually I use white vinegar, but lemon juice will work too. You just don't want to use something colored like balsamic vinegar or it will tint your eggs (however, in a pinch, this will work too). You want to add enough acid so that as soon as the whites hit the water, they begin to coagulate into a nice tight package—but you don't want them to smell (or taste!) like you're dying Easter eggs.

Poaching is a very GENTLE cooking method, unlike boiling, which is a very VIOLENT cooking method. If you try to poach eggs in boiling water, you will end up with egg drop soup. As an insurance policy, and to make sure the water is the proper temperature, take a pot of water and bring it to a boil (BTB). Turn the heat down until all the bubbles go away. Then, to drop your eggs into the poaching liquid, get very close to the surface of the water—this way you won't break your yolks!

Hey, did you know you can even poach eggs ahead of time? It's easy: Follow the directions above and once the eggs are cooked, hold them in a bowl of cool water until ready to serve. Then simply rewarm them in a pot of barely simmering water.

5 Gently crack the eggs into the poaching liquid and cook for 4 minutes. When they're done, the whites will be cooked through and the yolks will be warm and runny. While the eggs are cooking, toss the arugula in a large bowl with the lemon juice, a drizzle of big fat finishing oil, and a pinch of salt. TASTE IT and reseason if needed; the salad should be very flavorful but not soggy. Arrange the dressed arugula on serving plates and top with the porcini.

6 Remove the eggs from the poaching liquid with a slotted spoon and make a pit stop on a paper or tea towel to remove any excess water (you don't want to sog up your salad).

7 Lay a poached egg on top of the porcini and arugula, give each a sprinkey-dink of Parm, a pinch of red pepper, a bit of lemon zest, and a drizzle of big fat finishing oil. Serve with the grilled bread.

Voilà!

HEIRLOOM TOMATO SALAD

WITH WARM GOAT CHEESE

SERVES: 4 TO 6 · TIME: ABOUT 20 MINUTES

I look forward to tomato season all year—then when it comes, I always eat too many and practically overdose on them! But what's better than tomatoes with olive oil, vinegar, and a little salt? Tomatoes with goat cheese! What more can I say about an in-season heirloom tomato salad with other fabulous summer stuff thrown in? It's perfection.

MISE EN PLACE

1 8- to 10-ounce log of goat cheese

2 cups baby arugula

¼ cup red wine vinegar

¼ cup big fat finishing oil

Kosher salt

2 pounds heirloom tomatoes, different sizes, shapes, and colors, cut into wedges or slices

1 small red onion, finely julienned

6 or 7 fresh basil leaves, cut into a chiffonade (see page 58)

1 Preheat the oven to 375°F.

2 Put the goat cheese in a small ovenproof dish and bake for 8 to 10 minutes or until the cheese is warm, very soft, and slightly oozy.

3 While the cheese warms, toss the arugula in a medium bowl with 1 tablespoon each red wine vinegar and finishing oil, and season with salt. Divide the arugula between four serving plates.

4 In large bowl toss the tomatoes, onion, and basil with the remaining oil and vinegar and season with salt. Arrange the tomato mixture on top of the arugula and garnish each plate with a dollop of the warm goat cheese.

Holy tomato!

GRILLED SHRIMP
WITH CHICKPEA FRIES, ZUCCHINI & PINE NUT SALAD

SERVES: 4 · TIME: ABOUT 2 HOURS, MOSTLY UNATTENDED

There are so many things to love about chickpea fries—for starters you can make the base for this dish ahead of time and then fry up the fries just before you want to serve them. Also, I've added some crunched-up chickpeas into the mix for texture. And who ever thought of pairing these lovelies with a raw zucchini and onion salad? Look at me—always thinking up something new! Add a couple of grilled shrimp and some pine nuts, and you have something really special.

MISE EN PLACE

FOR THE CHICKPEA FRIES
Kosher salt

½ cup chickpea flour

½ teaspoon ground cumin

¼ teaspoon cayenne pepper

1 cup canned or cooked chickpeas, crushed

Extra virgin olive oil

FOR THE SALAD
8 jumbo shrimp, peeled and deveined (I prefer the ones with the head on)

Extra virgin olive oil

Kosher salt

1 zucchini, green part only, julienned

½ red onion, sliced super-thin

2 cups baby arugula

½ cup pine nuts, toasted (see page 17)

Juice of 2 lemons

FOR THE CHICKPEA FRIES

1 Put 2 cups water in a small saucepan, salt well, and bring to a boil (BTB) over high heat. Reduce the heat to low, whisk in the chickpea flour, and cook over low heat for 3 to 4 minutes, or until the mixture begins to thicken. Toss in the cumin, cayenne, and crushed chickpeas. When it's done, the mixture will be thick like mashed potatoes, about 15 minutes. Taste it—it should be REALLY good; if it isn't, reseason.

2 Spread the mixture out in a lightly oiled 9-inch baking dish and chill until fully set, at least an hour (this can be done in advance).

3 Cut the chilled mix into thick sticks, ¾ to 1 inch wide. Coat a nonstick sauté pan with olive oil and bring to high heat. While the oil heats, set up your drying situation next to the stove by putting a couple layers of paper towels on a baking sheet. Working in batches, cook the fries on all sides until golden and crispy, 3 to 4 minutes per side. Remove and drain on the paper towels, sprinkle with salt, and keep warm in a low oven.

FOR THE SALAD

1 Preheat a grill.

2 In a medium bowl, toss the shrimp with olive oil to coat and season with salt.

3 Put the zucchini, onion, arugula, and pine nuts in a large bowl and toss with lemon juice and olive oil. Season with salt and make sure it tastes delicious!

4 Grill the shrimp, turning once, until no longer translucent, 4 to 6 minutes total.

5 Arrange the salad on serving plates and top each with a couple of chickpea fries and 2 shrimp.

Chickpea-sy!

When you go to a fish store you might see numbers next to the shrimp. These numbers correlate to how many shrimp are in a pound (for example, 12/15 means there are between twelve and fifteen shrimp in a pound). The bigger the number, the more shrimp per pound; the smaller the number, the bigger the shrimp! For this recipe I recommend really big shrimp.

ANNE ALTERNATE

These chickpea fries are also really good with aïoli—check out the recipe on page 82 for a Q&E (quick and easy) dipper for these lovelies!

GRILLED
SEA SCALLOPS
WITH A WATERMELON THREE-WAY
& DANDELION GREENS

SERVES: 4 · TIME: ABOUT 1½ HOURS, MOSTLY UNATTENDED

I don't think there's anything terribly exciting about grilled scallops—but I do think you can put them together with interesting ingredients and *make* them exciting. That's why I pair scallops with—wait for it—watermelon! I know, who would think of putting scallops with watermelon, let alone three kinds (watermelon, watermelon rind pickles, and watermelon radishes)? It may seem wacky, but the sweetness of the watermelon offset by the bitterness of the dandelion and the sharp red onion makes this a spectacular combo.

And, if you're thinking ahead (like we always try to do!), make the pickles a day (or a week) in advance and keep them in the fridge. These pickles make anything taste tangy and delicious; I keep a jar on hand for whenever a salad or sammie needs an extra little pickle-y punch!

MISE EN PLACE

1-pound wedge watermelon

1 cup champagne or white wine vinegar

2 tablespoons sugar

2 tablespoons kosher salt, plus more for seasoning

Pinch of crushed red pepper

8 large sea scallops

2 to 3 tablespoons extra virgin olive oil, plus more as needed

1 watermelon radish (about the size of a kiwi), peeled and julienned

1 cup dandelion greens, cut into ½-inch-wide ribbons

½ small red onion, thinly sliced

1 Carefully cut the rind off the watermelon. Using a mandoline or a sharp vegetable peeler, shave the rind into wide ribbons about ⅛ inch thick. In a large bowl, combine the vinegar, sugar, salt, and red pepper. Add the watermelon rind ribbons and let stand at room temperature for at least an hour (BTW—this can totally be done yesterday).

2 Meanwhile, dice the watermelon flesh into ½-inch pieces and reserve.

3 When the watermelon pickles are done, heat the grill.

4 Brush the scallops with olive oil and season with salt. Place on the grill and cook until grill marks appear, about 1 minute, then rotate the scallops 90 degrees and let the grill marks develop in the other direction (what you're going for here are those lovely crosshatch grill marks!). Turn the scallops over and repeat; the scallops are done when they're no longer translucent, about 2 minutes each side.

5 While the scallops cook, drain the rind pickles, reserving their liquid. Toss the reserved watermelon, the rind pickles, watermelon radish, dandelion greens, and red onion together in a large bowl. Dress the salad with 2 tablespoons of the pickling liquid and some olive oil. TASTE! Adjust seasonings and dressing if needed.

6 Arrange the deliciously dressed salad in a tall pile just off the center of four salad plates. Cut the scallops equatorially (through the middle, like the equator) and lay the disks slightly overlapping, grilled side up, on the salad. Drizzle with a little olive oil.

Nice melons!

GRILLED
SOFT-SHELL
CRABS
WITH ASPARAGUS, ARUGULA & SPRING ONION SALAD WITH AÏOLI

SERVES: 4 · TIME: ABOUT 30 MINUTES

When soft-shell crabs are in season, it's the one time of year I like being crabby! I adore these guys perched on a delicious veggie salad with garlic mayo. The beauty of the soft-shell crab is you can eat the whole shootin' match—on a salad, in a sandwich, however. Who says being crabby isn't fun?

MISE EN PLACE

FOR THE AÏOLI
2 egg yolks
2 cloves garlic, smashed
3 tablespoons red wine vinegar
Kosher salt

1½ cups peanut or other neutral-flavored oil

FOR THE CRABS AND SALAD
4 soft-shell crabs
1 bunch of pencil or standard asparagus, tough bottom stems removed

Extra virgin olive oil
Kosher salt
2 cups baby arugula
2 spring onions, julienned
1 to 2 tablespoons red wine vinegar
1 to 2 tablespoons big fat finishing oil

FOR THE AÏOLI

Combine the egg yolks, garlic, vinegar, and a sprinkle of salt in the bowl of a food processor and purée until the mixture is homogeneous. Then, with the machine running, VERY slowly drizzle in the oil until it begins to thicken. When the mixture starts to look like mayonnaise, add the oil in a thin, slow stream. Check the aïoli for texture and flavor: If it's too thick, add a few drops of water to thin it; or on the flip side if it's too thin, add more oil. (This will make more than you need for this dish, so refrigerate the rest and use it on other good stuff, like the chickpea fries on page 78.)

FOR THE CRABS AND SALAD

1 Preheat the grill.

2 Clean the crabs by lifting up the outer shell on each side and pulling out the gills. Then pull the "apron" flap off the bottom of the crab. Using a sharp pair of scissors or kitchen shears, cut off the face and all the pointy parts of the shell. (I know this may seem mean; accept it and move on.) Pat the crabs with paper towels to remove all excess water.

3 In a large bowl, toss the asparagus with olive oil and salt. Rub the crabs with olive oil and sprinkle them with salt. Put the asparagus on the grill and cook, turning it occasionally, until charred and pliable, 7 to 8 minutes. Then put the crabs on the grill and cook for 3 to 4 minutes on each side or until firm. Remove the asparagus and crabs when done and set aside.

4 In a large bowl, toss together the arugula, spring onions, vinegar, and big fat finishing oil; season with salt and taste to make sure it's delicious.

5 Divide the dressed salad and asparagus between serving plates, top each with a soft-shell crab, and garnish each crab with a dollop of the delightful aïoli.

Got soft-shell crabs?!?

soft-shell crabs usually have a lot of water in them. be sure to pat them dry with paper towels to squeeze out any excess water before cooking.

SPICED CHICKPEA SOUP

WITH CRISPY, CRUNCHY CROUTONS

SERVES: 6 TO 8 · TIME: ABOUT 3 HOURS, NOT INCLUDING SOAKING TIME

I'm a bean lover but chickpeas are my favorite, so I make them the star of this spicy, satisfying rustic soup. I top off this bowl of comfort with some crispy, crunchy croutons and a drizzle of big fat finishing oil, and it takes me right back to Tuscany!

MISE EN PLACE

Extra virgin olive oil

1 large onion, peeled and cut into large dice

2 celery ribs, cut into ¼-inch dice

2 carrots, cut into ¼-inch dice

Kosher salt

2 pinches of crushed red pepper

6 cloves garlic, smashed

3 sprigs of fresh rosemary, leaves finely chopped

1 tablespoon cumin seeds, toasted and ground (see page 17)

1½ teaspoons coriander seeds, toasted and ground (see page 17)

1 pound dried chickpeas, soaked overnight (see page 55)

2 quarts chicken or veggie stock, plus more as needed

2 bay leaves

6 ½-inch slices stale rustic Italian bread, cut into ½-inch cubes

Big fat finishing oil

ANNE ALERT!

This recipe is best when you cook your own beans, so plan ahead.

1 Coat the bottom of a large pot with olive oil and add the onion, celery, and carrots. Season with salt and a pinch of red pepper. Bring to medium heat and cook the veggies for 7 to 8 minutes or until they begin to soften. Toss in half of the garlic, half of the rosemary, and the cumin and coriander, and cook for 3 to 4 minutes more.

2 Drain the chickpeas and add them to the pot along with the stock, bay leaves, and 2 cups water. Bring the liquid to a boil (BTB), reduce to a simmer (RTS), and cook for 1½ to 2 hours; at this point the chickpeas should be very soft. Turn off the heat and season the cooking liquid with salt; taste to make sure it's delicious and reseason if needed.

TAKING STOCK OF MAKING STOCK

I have found, through the course of my travels, that home cooks are scared to death of stock, which is totally ridiculous because it's one of the easiest things to make. With my foolproof method in hand, you should never have to reach for a can or a box of it again (unless in a super-pinch). So here's how it goes: Put carrots, onions, celery, and garlic in a large pot with a little oil, then sweat over medium heat for 7 to 8 minutes or until they start to soften. Add chicken legs and thighs, skin and fat removed. Fill the pot with water and then BTB, RTS, STS (bring to a boil, reduce to a simmer, skim the scum).

What do I mean by scum? Well, sometimes you may see some foam and fat on the surface of the stock. My Italian chef friends don't bother to remove it, they just cook it right back in; it gives the stock more flavor. I have a tendency to agree with this approach, but if you want to be a purist—go for it, skim away. Then simmer the stock for 2 hours, strain it, put it in your recycled Chinese soup containers, toss it in the freezer, and use it for whatever the heck you want to. THAT my friends, is how you make stock.

3 Coat the bottom of a skillet with olive oil and add the remaining garlic, rosemary, and pinch of red pepper. Bring to medium heat and add the bread, cooking until the cubes become golden and crispy, 6 to 8 minutes. Remove the croutons from the oil, drain on paper towels, and sprinkle with salt. These little guys will absorb a LOT of oil, but if there is any left in the pan, add it to the pot with the chickpeas.

4 Working in batches, purée the soup in a blender or food processor (OR you can use my favorite piece of kitchen equipment—the food mill) until very smooth. If the soup is too thin for your taste, cook it down; if it's too thick, add a bit more stock. Taste to make sure the seasoning is perfect, then ladle the soup into serving bowls, top with the croutons, and add a drizzle of big fat finishing oil.

See ya ladle!

OYSTERS
ON THE HALF SHELL
WITH PROSECCO "SNO-CONE"

SERVES: 4 · TIME: ABOUT 2 HOURS, MOSTLY UNATTENDED

This dish is SOOOOO titillating. When you eat these oysters you almost don't know which direction to turn. The intertwining flavors, textures, and temperatures come together to create a flavor explosion in your mouth. This is one *sexy* dish.

MISE EN PLACE

2 cups Prosecco or other bubbly wine

½ cup champagne or white wine vinegar

1 tablespoon finely chopped shallots

1 clove garlic, smashed and finely chopped

Pinch of crushed red pepper

1 tablespoon sugar

2 teaspoons kosher salt

2 teaspoons fresh thyme leaves

12 oysters, the freshest available (your favorite variety or a mix)

2 cups rock salt for plating (optional)

1 In a small saucepan combine the Prosecco, vinegar, shallots, garlic, red pepper, sugar, and kosher salt and bring to medium heat. Stir to be sure that all of the sugar and salt have dissolved. Remove from the heat and stir in the thyme.

2 Pour the mixture into a wide flat dish (such as a pie plate) and put it in the freezer. As the mixture begins to freeze, drag a fork through it to break up the ice crystals. Repeat this process every 15 minutes or so until the mixture is completely frozen, 45 minutes to 1 hour. When it's done it will look like ice shards, kind of like a slushy but a bit more frozen.

3 Scrub the outside of the oysters to remove any sand and grit. If you're using the rock salt, spread it out on a serving dish. Shuck the oysters and lay them on the salt; top each oyster with the icy granita and serve immediately.

This is the money shot!

A PEARL OF WISDOM ABOUT OYSTERS

When buying oysters, the same rules apply as when buying other shellfish (see page 67). To prepare them, you want to scrub the oysters well to remove any crud or grit. And to make shucking easy, you want to keep the oysters nice and cold. When shucking oysters ALWAYS use an oyster knife—never a paring knife. If you use a paring knife you WILL cut yourself, trust me.

I find this is the easiest way to shuck an oyster: Fold a clean tea towel into thirds lengthwise, lay the oyster on the towel, and fold the towel over the oyster to get a good grip. Lay your hand across the oyster with your thumb next to your palm, not spread across the oyster—if your thumb is spread across the oyster and you slip, you'll stab yourself. Yikes! With the oyster knife, find the little notch in the smaller end of the oyster where the knife fits in perfectly. Slow and steady wins the race here. Apply steady, even pressure and give the knife a slight twist; the top flat shell will pop and shift—so satisfying! Cup the oyster shell in your hand, being careful not to spill any of the liquor, and with your knife gently work to separate the oyster from the top shell; remove and discard the top. Slide the knife under the oyster so it releases from the bottom shell, then let it snuggle back into place. This technique makes for a diner-friendly oyster-eating experience!

PUMPKIN SOUP

WITH ALLSPICE WHIPPED CREAM & FRIED LEEKS

SERVES: 4 TO 6 · TIME: ABOUT 1 HOUR

I love this soup because it's my favorite color and the garnishes bump up the fancy factor! It's also totally seasonal—what could be more autumnal than a pretty pumpkin soup with spiced whipped cream and crispy leeks?

MISE EN PLACE

FOR THE SOUP

Extra virgin olive oil

2 leeks, white and light green parts only, cut in half lengthwise, washed, and diced

1 large or 2 small carrots, cut into ½-inch dice

2 celery ribs, cut into ½-inch dice

2 cloves garlic, smashed and finely chopped

Kosher salt

2 pounds pumpkin, peeled and cut into 1-inch dice (I recommend a sugar or cheese pumpkin, or in a pinch, butternut squash)

1 large russet potato, peeled and cut into 1-inch dice

2 cups white wine

2 quarts chicken or veggie stock

1 thyme bundle, tied with butcher's twine

2 bay leaves

1 orange, cut in half

FOR THE FRIED LEEKS

Canola or other neutral-flavored oil, for frying

1 leek, cut into 2-inch julienne, washed

Kosher salt

FOR THE WHIPPED CREAM

1 cup heavy cream

½ teaspoon allspice

FOR THE SOUP

1 Coat a large, deep pot with olive oil; add the leeks, carrots, celery, and garlic and bring to medium-high heat. Season with salt and sweat the veggies until they start to soften and are very aromatic, 8 to 10 minutes. Add the pumpkin and potato and sprinkle with salt. Stir to coat the mixture with the oil and cook for another 5 to 6 minutes; add the wine and reduce by half.

2 Add the stock, thyme bundle, and bay leaves. Squeeze the orange halves directly into the soup, then add both halves. Taste for seasoning and adjust if needed. Bring to a boil (BTB) and reduce to a simmer (RTS); cook for 35 to 40 minutes.

3 Remove and discard the orange halves, thyme bundle, and bay leaves and use an immersion blender or upright blender to purée the soup (if you're using a regular blender, cool the mixture for about 5 minutes and work in batches). You want the purée to be very smooth and velvety, so purée the crap out of it! If the consistency is too thick, add a bit of water. Taste and adjust the seasoning as needed.

FOR THE FRIED LEEKS

Heat an inch of oil in a small saucepan set over medium heat. While the oil heats, set up your drying situation next to the stove by putting a couple layers of paper towels on a baking sheet. When the oil is hot, working in batches, fry the leeks until crispy and brown, 2 to 4 minutes. Use a slotted spoon or fish spatula to remove the leeks and set them on the paper towels to drain; sprinkle with salt.

TO WHIP THE CREAM AND SERVE

1 Use a hand or stand mixer—or if you're feeling strong, a regular old whisk—to whip the cream and allspice until the cream holds its shape in soft peaks (see page 234).

2 Ladle the soup into serving bowls, top with a dollop of the whipped cream, and garnish with the fried leeks.

Soup-er!!!

RAW ASPARAGUS, RED ONION
& PECORINO SALAD

SERVES: 6 TO 8 · TIME: ABOUT 10 MINUTES

This is one of my best recipes (if I do say so myself!) and it's become one of my mom's favorites, too. People will say, "What is this?" and then, "Who knew you could eat raw asparagus?" It's simple and unique and, I promise, it will make you a rock star with your guests.

MISE EN PLACE

1 bunch of pencil asparagus, tough bottom stems removed

1 small red onion, finely diced

1 cup finely grated Pecorino

¼ to ½ cup red wine vinegar

Big fat finishing oil

Kosher salt

1 Cut the asparagus, including the tips, into very thin rounds. In a medium bowl, toss the asparagus with the red onion and Pecorino.

2 Drizzle the salad with the vinegar (I like a very bright, acidic salad, but you can adjust the vinegar to your taste), finishing oil, and salt and toss again.

Super-cinchy!

ROASTED BEET
& MANY-HERB SALAD

SERVES: 4 · TIME: 1 HOUR, MOSTLY UNATTENDED

Everyone makes a big production over roasting beets when the truth is that you can literally throw them in the oven—no foil, no nothing, totally naked—and let them do their thing. Combine those beautiful beets with lovely fresh herbs and you get a gorgeous salad with different flavors in every bite. Who knew beets could be so exciting?

MISE EN PLACE

4 large beets, red, golden, Chioggia, or any combination

8 to 10 baby beets, any color or combination

3 tablespoons balsamic vinegar

3 tablespoons extra virgin olive oil

Kosher salt

2 cups mixed fresh herbs (parsley, dill, chives, basil, fennel fronds, marjoram, oregano, and/or thyme), leaves pinched from stems

1 Preheat the oven to 375°F.

2 Place the large beets on a baking sheet large enough to hold the small ones as well and roast for 20 minutes. Add the baby beets to the baking sheet and roast until all the beets are fork-tender, another 20 to 25 minutes. When all the beets are cooked through, remove them from the oven (they should be done at the same time).

3 When they're cool enough to handle, peel the beets (you may want to use paper towels to avoid staining your hands). Slice the large beets into ½-inch slices and cut the baby beets in half.

4 Place all the beets in a large bowl, toss with 2 tablespoons vinegar and 2 tablespoons olive oil, and season with salt. Arrange the assorted beets on salad plates. Put all the herbs in a bowl and dress lightly with the remaining vinegar and oil. Season with salt and TASTE! If you like your salad really well dressed, go ahead and up the amount of oil and vinegar in equal parts—remember, train your palate and trust your own sense of taste.

Can't beet that!

> To know when the beets are done, just stick a fork in them—notice that in the recipe I say "fork-tender," not "paring-knife tender." A knife is sharp and will slide in and out easily even if the beets aren't fully cooked. A fork, on the other hand, is dull and won't slide in and out unless the beets are totally done.

MY BIG FAT
CHICKEN
SOUP

SERVES: 6 TO 8 · TIME: ABOUT 1¾ HOURS

Chicken soup is so comforting on so many levels, and it's a cinch to whip up a pot of your own rather than opening a can (which is not that healthy, by the way). And here's a tip: If you're going to make a little, you might as well make a lot and toss the leftovers in the freezer.

MISE EN PLACE

Extra virgin olive oil

1 large onion, cut into ½-inch dice

4 celery ribs, cut into ½-inch dice

3 carrots, cut into ½-inch dice

Kosher salt

2 cloves garlic, smashed

2 teaspoons crushed red pepper

1 thyme bundle, tied with butcher's twine

3 pounds bone-in chicken legs and thighs, skin and excess fat removed

2 bay leaves

1 lemon, halved

1 teaspoon cinnamon

2 grates of fresh nutmeg

Freshly ground black pepper

1 15-ounce can white beans or chickpeas, drained and rinsed

1 cup corn kernels (frozen is fine)

1 bunch of fresh cilantro, leaves coarsely chopped

1 Coat a large stockpot with olive oil and add the onion, celery, and carrots. Season with salt and bring to medium heat. Cook the vegetables until they start to soften and are very aromatic, 8 to 10 minutes. Add the garlic, red pepper, and thyme bundle and cook for another 2 to 3 minutes. Add the chicken and bay leaves and fill the pot with enough water to cover everything; bring to a boil (BTB), then reduce to a simmer (RTS).

2 Cook for 30 minutes, then skim the scum or foam that may accumulate on the surface. Squeeze the lemon halves into the soup, then drop in the halves. Add the cinnamon and nutmeg and taste; season with salt if needed and let the soup simmer for another hour.

3 Take the soup off the heat and discard the lemon halves, thyme bundle, and bay leaves. Remove the chicken from the broth and let it cool. When the chicken is cool enough to handle, remove the bones, pull the meat into bite-size pieces, and add it back to the pot. Taste the soup for seasoning—it should be spicy with a bright lemony kick and a warm cinnamon flavor.

4 Add the beans to the pot along with the corn; let the soup continue to cook over low heat until the beans are warmed through. Taste again for seasoning, adjust if needed, and garnish with cilantro to serve.

That's what I call chicken soup for the soul!

PARMIGIANO FLAN

SERVES: 6 · TIME: ABOUT 40 MINUTES

I call these my little Parmigiano puddings and when I say they are easy to pull together, I'm SOOOOO not kidding. They're also easily made ahead of time—in fact, I recommend doing so—and they're a huge crowd pleaser at a party. Just put them in a 300°F oven for 5 to 7 minutes to take the chill off before serving.

MISE EN PLACE

FOR THE FLAN

Nonstick cooking spray

2 cups heavy cream

4 large eggs

1 cup freshly grated Parmigiano

Kosher salt

Pinch of cayenne

FOR THE SALAD

1 bunch pencil asparagus, tough bottom stems removed

Extra virgin olive oil

Kosher salt

Pinch of crushed red pepper

2 cups arugula or mesclun

½ red onion, thinly sliced

Big fat finishing oil

Zest and juice of 1 lemon

FOR THE FLAN

1 Preheat the oven to 325°F.

2 Spray six 4-ounce ramekins or disposable aluminum cups with nonstick spray. In a large bowl, combine the cream, eggs, Parm, salt, and cayenne and whisk well. Taste for seasoning and adjust as needed. Divide the mixture evenly between the ramekins.

3 Put the ramekins in a baking dish large enough to hold them all, then fill the dish with hot water until it reaches halfway up the sides of the ramekins—be careful here, you don't want any water getting in the ramekins! Cover the dish with aluminum foil and bake for 30 to 35 minutes, or until the flans are set. Remove from the oven and let the dish cool on a rack.

FOR THE SALAD

1 Heat the oven to 400°F.

2 Toss the asparagus with olive oil until lightly coated and sprinkle with salt and red pepper. Put on a baking sheet and cook for 7 to 10 minutes, or until it begins to color and is pliable.

3 In a large bowl toss the arugula, asparagus, and red onion with finishing oil, lemon zest, juice, and salt. Taste and adjust the seasoning.

TO SERVE

To unmold the flans, gently run a butter knife around the outside edge of each ramekin, then flip them over onto serving plates, slightly off center. To serve, arrange the salad so it leans up against the flan.

Flan-tastic!

SUGAR SNAP PEA SALAD

WITH CRISPY PROSCIUTTO & MINT

SERVES: 4 · TIME: ABOUT 15 MINUTES

I love sugar snaps because they're crispy, they're crunchy, and they're snappy! Just blanch, shock, and cut them into little slivers to enjoy the full sugar snappy experience. To keep things interesting, toss in some minty fresh deliciousness and some salty, crispy prosciutto! Now that's what I call a summertime salad.

MISE EN PLACE

Kosher salt

1 pound sugar snap peas, stem ends and strings removed

Extra virgin olive oil

1 clove garlic, smashed

Pinch of crushed red pepper

¼ pound prosciutto, sliced thin and cut crosswise into ¼-inch strips

¼ cup red wine vinegar

2 cups baby arugula

½ small red onion, julienned

¼ cup Pecorino, shaved with a veggie peeler

8 to 10 fresh mint leaves, cut into a chiffonade (see page 58)

1 To blanch the peas, bring a large pot of well-salted water to a boil and set up a large bowl of well-salted ice water. Toss the peas into the boiling water, let the water return to a boil, and cook for 2 more minutes. Remove the peas from the boiling water and immediately plunge them into the ice water. When the peas are cold, drain them and lay on paper towels to dry.

2 Cut the peas in half lengthwise and reserve.

3 Coat a medium sauté pan with olive oil and add the garlic and red pepper; bring the pan to medium heat and cook for 2 to 3 minutes. Remove the garlic and ditch it—it has fulfilled its garlic destiny! Add the prosciutto to the pan and cook for 3 to 4 minutes or until crispy, then add the vinegar. Turn off the heat.

4 In a large bowl, combine the arugula, snap peas, and onion along with the prosciutto and any juices from the pan; toss well. Add the Pecorino and mint and TASTE it! Season with salt if needed and serve.

That's snappy!

sugar snap peas often have strings that run along
the edge of the pod - be sure to remove them because
eating sugar snaps and flossing at the same time is
not a pleasant experience!

3

PASTA

{ my passion }

Pasta is my favorite thing to make, cook, and eat. Sure, I LOOOOOVE to cook almost anything, but I LOVE-PLUS pasta. It's the food that really speaks to me. My passion for pasta started as a teenager when I was given one of the old-fashioned Atlas hand-crank pasta machines for Christmas—long before I ever decided to become a professional chef. I spent a lot of time playing with that machine, and back then it took me far longer than it should have to make a pound of pasta. Now, after doing it for years, I've got it down—I can whip right through it.

TO THIS DAY THERE'S STILL NOTHING IN COOKING AS THRILLING TO ME as mixing together some flour, oil, eggs, and water and imagining all the possibilities, all the delicious things I can create—and with such basic ingredients! On *Iron Chef,* when I'm working with Mario, my main job is making the pasta, and I have to make it really fast and absolutely perfect EVERY TIME. And guess what? My thousands of pounds of pasta practice are going to help streamline this operation for you—so get ready!

But before you jump in and start whipping up a bowl of carbonara, there's something you have to understand: Pasta deserves respect. It's not mashed potatoes; you don't serve it as a side dish. PASTA IS ITS OWN COURSE. And you don't pile a plate with mounds of spaghetti covered in red sauce. You eat small portions of pasta that have been lovingly tossed with a delicious sauce to create the perfect marriage. Sometimes in Italy you'll be served multiple pasta courses, but they're always small so you can savor the flavors and enjoy how the noodles and sauce work together. Remember, pasta is its own special thing, and it needs to be treated that way.

This is true when it comes to cooking the pasta as well. It's not just about boiling some salted water and tossing in the noodles; it's about how you cook the noodle, about the aroma and consistency of the pasta when it's done, the scent of the sauce, and the taste of the two together once they're intertwined in the bowl. Every sauce acts differently— cream sauces are totally different from vegetable sauces; seafood sauces are completely unlike meat sauces. Yes, they're all condiments to go with the pasta, but they each bring something sparkly and wonderful and all their own to the party.

Knowing how to make pasta—and make it well—is an essential part of Italian cooking. Endless dishes can be created around pasta, and once you know how to make it the right way, you'll never be at a loss for something delicious to eat.

Chef Anne's All-Purpose Pasta Dough

Chef Anne's Light-as-a-Cloud Gnocchi

Wild Mushroom Ragù

Sweet & Spicy Sausage Ragù

Pasta Carbonara

Pasta Fagioli

Bucatini all'Amatriciana

Raviolo al'Uovo (Ricotta-Nestled Egg Yolk)

Spaghetti with Olive-Oil-Poached Tuna
in Tomato-Fennel Sauce

Tagliolini with Arugula-Walnut Sauce

Spag & Excellent "Meatbawls"

Tagliatelle with Bacon, Sweet Corn,
Burst Cherry Tomatoes & Arugula

Tagliolini with Salsa Cruda & Ricotta Salata

Orecchiette with Broccoli Rabe Pesto & Sausage

Spring Pea & Ricotta Ravioli with Fava Beans

Whole Wheat Pappardelle with Roasted Butternut Squash,
Broccoli Rabe & Pumpkin Seeds

Spinach & Ricotta Gnocchi with Fontina Fonduta

Chef Anne's Risotto-Without-a-Recipe

Risotto with Rock Shrimp, Lemon & Herbs

Farrotto with Lobster, Peas, Mint & Oregano

Killer Mac & Cheese with Bacon

PASTA DOUGH

SERVES: 4 TO 6 · TIME: ABOUT 2 HOURS

Making fresh pasta doesn't have to be a big to-do. Yes, it can be a lot of work, but the possibilities that await you are endlessly exciting. I love what can be done with just a few basic ingredients and a little bit of skill. Depending on the season, the amount of time you have, or the mood you're in, you can make short pasta, long pasta, stuffed pasta, whatever you like. As your skill and confidence grow, you'll realize that a whole new world is open to you with fresh pasta. What I offer here is a way for you to dip your toe in the pool of well-salted pasta water and see where the noodles take you!

MISE EN PLACE

1 pound all-purpose flour (about 3¾ cups), plus more for dusting

4 large eggs plus 1 yolk
¼ cup extra virgin olive oil

Kosher salt

1 Mound the flour on a clean, dry work surface. Make a big hole (called a well) in the center of the flour pile—bigger is definitely better here. Crack the eggs into the hole along with the extra yolk, olive oil, and 2 tablespoons water; season with salt. Using a fork, beat the eggs together with the olive oil, water, and salt and begin to incorporate the flour into the egg mixture. Be careful not to break the well or the egg mixture will run everywhere and you'll have a big fat mess on your hands (and your board). When enough flour is incorporated that you can handle the dough, use your hands to combine everything really well. If the mixture is tight and dry, wet your hands a bit. When the mixture is homogeneous, start kneading . . .

2 To knead the dough, it's VERY important to put your body weight into it, to get on top of the dough, and really stretch it. Be careful not to tear it—the idea is that you stretch the

dough, not rip it. Use the heels of your palms and roll the mixture over itself. When it's done it should be smooth, supple, and velvety and look like the head of a preemie Cabbage Patch doll. Kneading will take anywhere from 8 to 15 minutes, depending on how experienced you are. (Don't hold back: This is where the perfect, toothsome texture of your pasta is formed. Get in there and work it!)

3 When the pasta is ready, wrap it in plastic and let it rest for at least an hour at room temperature before rolling. If you're making the dough ahead of time, wrap, refrigerate, and bring to room temperature before using.

4 To roll out pasta, you need to run the dough through the pasta roller a bunch of times to get it long and thin. To start, cut off about a quarter of the dough (remember, the bigger the piece you start with, the longer your dough is going to

get), keeping the rest wrapped up so it doesn't dry out. Squish the dough to flatten it—this will help it run through the pasta roller more easily. Where do we start? We start at the beginning! Run the dough through the pasta roller starting on the widest setting, number 1. Then dust the dough with flour, fold it into thirds, and put the dough through this setting two more times. If the dough ever feels sticky or tacky, give it a little dusting of flour. Now adjust the setting to number 2 and repeat the process again— changing the setting each time until your dough is the desired thickness. Once the dough is rolled out, be sure to keep the pasta sheets covered so they don't dry out. Depending on what I want to use the pasta for, I usually stop around number 5 or 6. For long noodles I keep it thicker, and for ravioli or stuffed pasta, I keep it thinner. All pasta machines are different, so you need to judge how your pasta machine works and adjust your rolling accordingly. Once you get the thickness you want, repeat this process with the remaining pieces of dough.

For whole wheat pasta, substitute 2 cups of whole wheat flour for 2 cups of the all-purpose white. Whole wheat flour is really dry, so you'll likely have to add some water. Start with ¼ cup water and see how it goes. You don't want tight, nervous-feeling dough, but how much water you need to add depends on what the flour is telling you that day.

MAKING FRESH PASTA . . . PERFECTLY

TYPE OF PASTA	MACHINE SETTING	DESIRED SIZE/SHAPE
Ravioli	Approximately 6–7	Thin pasta sheets
Pappardelle	Approximately 5–6	1-inch-wide ribbons
Tagliatelle	Approximately 5–6	¼-inch-wide ribbons
Tagliolini	Approximately 4-5	⅛-inch-wide ribbons

CHEF ANNE'S ALL-PURPOSE PASTA COOKING METHOD

Pasta needs to be cooked in lots of water that's salty like the ocean. Every single time I cook pasta I taste the water to make sure it's correctly seasoned. This step is imperative; if you don't season your pasta water correctly, it doesn't matter how good your sauce is, your pasta dish will never recover.

So here's what you need to do: Season your pasta water abundantly (as I said, like the ocean—not the Dead Sea!), bring it to a boil, add the pasta, and give it a good swish to make sure the pasta doesn't stick together. Don't crowd your pasta; it needs plenty of room to swim around.

You want dried pasta cooked al dente, which means "on the tooth," so cook it about one minute less than the package directions recommend (it's going to cook more once you add it to the sauce). When you bite into any well-cooked dried pasta, you should see a little nugget of hard pasta on the inside. It shouldn't be crunchy, but it should definitely have a toothsome bite.

Fresh pasta is a different story. It has not been dried so it's impossible to get that dry white center, and a limp noodle is no fun. Fresh pasta cooks very quickly, so it's essential to pay attention. What you're looking for is a noodle that's tender but also has that toothsome texture when you bite into it.

Once the pasta is cooked, whether fresh or dried, you need to perform the marriage of the pasta and sauce by draining the pasta and cooking it in the sauce for a couple minutes, until the sauce hugs the pasta. It's a good idea to always reserve a little of your pasta cooking water; you never know when you're going to need to loosen up your sauce, and this is the way to do it. As the pasta and sauce cook, give them a sprinkey-dink of grated Parm, a drizzle of big fat finishing oil, and stir or toss VIGOROUSLY. This is the glue that holds the marriage of the pasta and sauce together—they should cling to one another! Serve the pasta immediately, and know that proper etiquette is to start eating right away—don't wait for everyone to be served.

CHEF ANNE'S LIGHT-AS-A-CLOUD
GNOCCHI

SERVES: 10 TO 12 · TIME: ABOUT 3 HOURS, MOSTLY UNATTENDED

I've had a lot of bad gnocchi in my life. You know the kind I'm talking about: You eat three and suddenly your belly expands and you feel like balls of bread dough are rising in there. Gnocchi should be light and airy, like clouds! Over time I've perfected the secrets to great gnocchi and if you follow this recipe, even as a beginner, you will be successful EVERY time.

MISE EN PLACE

5 large Idaho potatoes

2 large eggs

¾ cup freshly grated Parmigiano, plus extra for garnish

Kosher salt

2 to 3 cups all-purpose flour (depending on humidity, this will range)

Big fat finishing oil

1 Preheat the oven to 375°F.

2 Put the potatoes on a baking sheet and cook until fork-tender, 45 minutes to 1 hour—check them along the way.

3 Line a rimmed baking sheet with parchment paper. While the potatoes are still hot, peel and pass them through a food mill or ricer, distributing them in a thin, even layer onto the baking sheet (personally I find that a food mill works better than a ricer because it's easier to handle). Keep the layer as light and fluffy as possible as you do this to help keep the gnocchi light. When they're thoroughly riced, put the baking sheet in the fridge and cool the potatoes completely. (If the potatoes are warm when you add the flour, they'll absorb more flour, leading to heavier gnocchi.)

4 When the potatoes are totally cold, dump them out on a clean work surface. In a small bowl, beat the eggs and cheese together and pour this mixture over the potatoes; season with salt.

5 Cover everything generously with flour—it should look like snow on the mountains—and crumble the potato-flour mixture between your fingers, kneading the dough until it's a homogeneous mixture. The dough should feel slightly moist, but not tacky. If it's too tacky, repeat the snow-on-the-mountains stage.

6 Form the dough into a large log. Cut 1-inch slices off the log and roll them into long ropes about ¾ inch thick. Cut the ropes into ½-inch lengths and cover generously with flour. Dust a baking sheet with flour and place the gnocchi on it in a single layer. (Do not even THINK of piling them on top of each other!)

RECIPE CONTINUES

7 Use or freeze the gnocchi immediately. (If freezing, put the baking sheet directly in the freezer. Once frozen, the gnocchi can be put in plastic bags and stored indefinitely. Frozen gnocchi can go directly from the freezer into salted boiling water.) When ready to cook, bring a large pot of well-salted water to a boil. Add the gnocchi and cook until they float to the top of the pot and get nice and puffy. Scoop the gnocchi out of the water, toss with whatever sauce you like, and finish with a little big fat finishing oil and grated Parm.

Gnocchi-dokee!

To make great gnocchi, remember these two secrets: When passing the potatoes through the food mill, keep them as light and fluffy as possible; don't let them get packed down. Also, it is a general practice to take gnocchi out of the water as soon as they float—BIG MISTAKE! Gnocchi need to be cooked in boiling water until they float *and* get nice and puffy. Don't be fooled; undercooking will result in heavy gnocchi.

WILD MUSHROOM
RAGÙ

SERVES: 4 TO 6 · TIME: ABOUT 1 HOUR

When I was working in Tuscany during porcini season I always wanted to go foraging for mushrooms, but the Italians are so secretive about where they find their prized porcini that I could never convince anyone to take me with them. So, while I never got to go hunting for fresh porcini, I did learn how to use dried ones to make this gorgeous sauce.

If you've never used them before, dried porcini are a fantastic way to add a huge bump of mushroomy goodness to almost anything. And, because you have to soak them first, you get the added benefit of the fastest, most flavorful vegetarian stock ever; one that you can then add to your sauce to give it an even richer, earthier boost of flavor—just like I do here.

MISE EN PLACE

½ cup dried porcini mushrooms

Extra virgin olive oil

1 onion, cut into ¼-inch dice

Pinch of crushed red pepper

Kosher salt

2 cloves garlic, smashed and finely chopped

2 pounds assorted fresh mushrooms (porcini, shiitake, oyster, and cremini are all great), trimmed, cleaned, and cut into bite-size pieces

1 cup dry white wine

1 to 2 cups chicken or veggie stock (see page 85)

1 thyme bundle, tied with butcher's twine

1 bay leaf

1 Soak the porcini in 3 cups hot water until very soft, about 30 minutes.

2 Coat a large wide saucepan generously with olive oil and bring to medium-high heat. Add the onion and red pepper and season with salt; cook until the onion is soft and aromatic, 8 to 10 minutes. Add the garlic and cook for 2 to 3 minutes more.

3 Add the fresh mushrooms, season with salt, and sauté until soft, 8 to 10 minutes. Add the wine and continue cooking until reduced by half, 5 to 6 minutes more.

4 Using your hand, scoop the porcini out of the soaking water, being careful not to disturb

the water—you want the crud to stay settled. Put the porcini in a food processor, ladle in about ½ cup of the soaking liquid, and purée to a very smooth paste.

5 Add the porcini paste, 2 cups of the porcini water, and 1 cup of the stock to the pan; toss in the thyme bundle and the bay leaf. Taste and season with salt if needed. Bring the liquid to a boil (BTB) and reduce to a simmer (RTS). Simmer for 25 to 30 minutes, adding more stock if needed; this sauce should be saucy but not soupy. Remove the thyme bundle and bay leaf before serving. Serve tossed with pasta or gnocchi or over polenta.

That's a wild funghi!

SWEET & SPICY
SAUSAGE
RAGÙ

SERVES: 4 TO 6 · TIME: ABOUT 4 HOURS, MOSTLY UNATTENDED

Years ago, I was working at a tiny restaurant in Tuscany. This is where I first learned to make ragù—an unbelievably delicious sauce that I would let cook for hours and hours. But in the beginning, no matter how long I let it simmer, the owner would come over, taste it, and tell me the vegetables were raw! In my head I remember thinking, are you freaking kidding me? But he was right. I was skimping on an essential step—I was rushing the browning of the soffritto: the early stage in a ragù's life cycle when the flavor begins to build and deepen. Now, of course, I'm super-sensitive to this step, and when I taste a ragù in a restaurant, I can tell instantly if the chef has taken a shortcut at the browning stage. So be patient—if you're taking the time and effort to make this spectacular sauce, don't rush it; *brown it* and enjoy!

MISE EN PLACE

2 onions, cut into 1-inch dice

1 small fennel bulb, tops and tough middle stalk removed, cut into 1-inch dice

2 celery ribs, cut into 1-inch dice

3 cloves garlic, smashed

Extra virgin olive oil

Kosher salt

2 cups tomato paste

2 cups hearty red wine

1 pound sweet Italian sausage, casings removed

1 pound spicy Italian sausage, casings removed

2 bay leaves

1 thyme bundle, tied with butcher's twine

1 pound spaghetti

½ to ¾ cup freshly grated Parmigiano

Big fat finishing oil

1 Put the onions, fennel, celery, and garlic in a food processor and purée to a coarse paste.

2 Coat a wide, deep pan with olive oil, add the puréed veggies, season with salt, and bring to medium-high heat. Cook the veggies until all the liquid has evaporated and they begin to stick to the pan—you want to brown the crap out of these guys until crud starts to form on the bottom of the pan. Stir occasionally to

scrape up the brown bits, then let the crud form again. Be patient here and don't rush it—this is where the big flavor develops—it will take up to 30 minutes.

3 When the lovely brown crud has formed and been scraped down a couple of times, add the tomato paste, stirring to combine. Let it start to

RECIPE CONTINUES

WELCOME TO THE DANCE!

The browning that takes place in the beginning of this ragù recipe—as for all sauces and braises—helps develop the deep, rich, brown flavors we want. Then the dance begins! By adding water and then reducing it, the brown flavors dance with the water, developing personality and complexity. If you add all the water in the beginning, the personality of the ragù will be watery and boring. If you don't add enough water, or the ragù isn't cooked long enough, the personality will be thick and one-dimensional. The dance should take about 3 hours. As you taste the ragù throughout the cooking process, you'll see the amazing changes in its personality. Stir occasionally, taste, season, and continue to add more water as the ragù cooks down. Enjoy the way your house smells—be patient and have fun!

brown a little and continue stirring for 2 to 3 minutes. There's not much liquid at this point to keep things from burning, so be careful and move fast. Add the wine, stir to combine, and scrape up any remaining brown bits; cook until about half the wine has evaporated, 4 to 5 minutes.

4 Add both the sweet and the spicy sausage and, using a spoon to break it up, cook until the meat is brown (this is where another round of big brown flavors is formed, so take your time), 10 to 15 minutes.

5 Add enough water to the pan to cover the meat by about ½ inch. Stir to combine well and add the bay leaves and the thyme bundle. Taste, season with salt, and taste again—it's by no means done, but it should taste good. Bring the sauce to a boil (BTB) and reduce to a simmer (RTS). Continue cooking, checking occasionally, for 3 hours, tasting, seasoning, and adding more water as needed (see above).

6 During the last half hour of the cooking process, bring a large pot of well-salted water to a boil. Add the pasta and cook for 1 minute less than the instructions on the package suggest. Taste it: It should be toothsome with just a little nugget of hard pasta still in the center—this is al dente. Drain, reserving ½ cup of the pasta cooking water. Remove the thyme bundle and bay leaf from the sauce. Then remove half of the ragù from the pan and reserve. Immediately add the cooked pasta to the pan with the ragù and toss to combine, adding more of the reserved ragù or pasta water if needed; continue cooking for another couple of minutes, until the pasta and sauce cling together and the liquid has reduced.

7 Remove the pot from the heat and add the Parmigiano and a generous drizzle of the big fat finishing oil. Toss the pasta and sauce vigorously—this is the marriage of the pasta and sauce, and the cheese and olive oil are the glue that holds this lovely relationship together.

Call yourself a superstar!

CARBONARA

SERVES: 4 TO 6 · TIME: ABOUT 30 MINUTES

Eggs, bacon, and cheese, oh my! After a long shift in the kitchen and a few glasses of wine, carbonara is a chef's late-night favorite. It's fast, flavorful, and oh-so-satisfying. The thing is, as much as I love it, carbonara poses a bit of a dichotomy for me because while it involves some of my very favorite ingredients (eggs, bacon, and cheese), it also includes my nemesis: black pepper. The thing is, this is such a classic preparation that black pepper really belongs here—so I use it.

MISE EN PLACE

Kosher salt
Extra virgin olive oil

¾ cup pancetta, cut into ¼-inch dice
1 pound spaghetti
8 large eggs
½ cup freshly grated Parmigiano

½ cup freshly grated Pecorino
Freshly ground black pepper
4 scallions, green parts only, cut into 1-inch lengths on a severe bias

1 Bring a large pot of well-salted water to a boil. Coat a large skillet with olive oil and bring it to medium heat. Add the pancetta and cook, stirring occasionally, until it starts to color and become crisp, 6 to 8 minutes; remove from the heat.

2 Add the pasta to the boiling water and cook for 1 minute less than the instructions on the package suggest. Taste it: It should be toothsome with just a little nugget of hard pasta still in the center—this is al dente.

3 While the pasta is cooking, crack the eggs into a large bowl and add the grated Parm and Pecorino; season with salt and whisk vigorously until well combined. Season with black pepper—seriously, this is one place where pepper brings something special to the party!

4 Bring the pan with the pancetta back to medium heat. Drain the pasta, add it to the pan, and coat it with any fat in the skillet. Remove the pan from the heat, add the egg mixture to the pasta, and stir vigorously to combine. Cover and let sit for 1 to 2 minutes so the steam gently cooks the eggs. Uncover and stir again—the egg mixture will seem like a cream sauce. Serve immediately garnished with sliced scallions.

Buonissimo!

a great carbonara is all about timing: render the pancetta, cook the pasta, and toss it all together while everything is screaming hot - this will ensure the eggs are cooked ever-so-gently.

PASTA FAGIOLI

SERVES: 4 TO 6 · TIME: ABOUT 1 HOUR

I love beans—any time, any way. And while my preference is to cook my own beans (see page 55), I'm the first to admit that sometimes a can of beans is a lifesaver. For this recipe in particular I have no problems using canned beans, and you shouldn't either. Having a few cans in the pantry means whipping up this dish is easy—it's one of my very favorite things to make when I want something super comforting to slurp up and stick to my belly while sitting around watching TV on a Sunday afternoon.

MISE EN PLACE

Extra virgin olive oil

¼ pound pancetta, cut into ¼-inch dice

1 onion, cut into ¼-inch dice

Kosher salt

Pinch of crushed red pepper

2 cloves garlic, smashed and finely chopped

1 28-ounce can San Marzano tomatoes, passed through a food mill

2 15-ounce cans cannellini beans, drained and rinsed

2 15-ounce cans chickpeas, drained and rinsed

1 pound ditalini pasta

Freshly grated Parmigiano

Big fat finishing oil

Chopped chives for garnish

1 Coat a large wide pot with olive oil and add the pancetta. Bring to medium heat and cook the pancetta until it starts to crisp, 4 to 5 minutes. Toss in the onion and season with salt and red pepper; cook until the onion is soft and aromatic, 8 to 10 minutes. Add the garlic and cook for 2 to 3 minutes more. Add the tomatoes and 1 cup water, season with salt, and bring to a boil (BTB); then reduce to a simmer (RTS) and cook for 15 minutes.

2 Add the cannellini beans and chickpeas to the pot and cook for 20 minutes more.

3 Bring a large pot of well-salted water to a boil. Cook the pasta two-thirds of the way—it should still be fairly hard in the middle. Drain the pasta, reserving 1 cup of the cooking water. Add the pasta and the reserved cooking water to the pot with the tomatoes and beans. Continue cooking until the pasta is done, another 3 to 4 minutes. Taste and adjust the seasoning if needed.

4 Serve sprinkled with Parm and chives and drizzled with big fat finishing oil.

Fagio-licious!

BUCATINI
ALL'AMATRICIANA

SERVES: 4 TO 6 · TIME: ABOUT 1½ HOURS

When I'm in the mood for tomato sauce, Amatriciana is my go-to. It's all about onions, spicy tomatoes, and pork products. Guanciale—cured pork jowl—is the key here. It has a sweeter, more interesting flavor than bacon. In a pinch, pancetta can be substituted, and in a double pinch bacon will suffice (though it does add a smokier flavor, so be warned). What else can I say? This sauce makes me want to dive into the bowl head first with my mouth wide open!

MISE EN PLACE

Extra virgin olive oil

8 ounces guanciale, cut into ¼-inch strips

4 onions, cut into ½-inch dice

½ to 1 teaspoon crushed red pepper

Kosher salt

2 28-ounce cans San Marzano tomatoes, passed through a food mill

1 pound bucatini or perciatelli

½ cup freshly grated Parmigiano, plus extra for garnish

Big fat finishing oil

1 Coat a large saucepan with olive oil; add the guanciale and cook over low heat until it's brown and crispy and has rendered a lot of fat, 6 to 8 minutes. Remove the guanciale and set a third of it aside for garnish—I like to call these bits "the crispy critters."

2 Bring the pan and the remaining fat to medium heat, add the onions and red pepper, and season generously with salt. Cook until the onions are soft and aromatic, 8 to 10 minutes.

3 Add the tomatoes and two-thirds of the guanciale, and bring to a boil (BTB), then reduce to a simmer (RTS) and cook the sauce for about 1 hour, tasting periodically and adding salt as needed (trust me, you will need to reseason).

4 Bring a large pot of well-salted water to a boil. Add the pasta and cook for 1 minute less than the instructions on the package suggest. Taste it:

It should be toothsome with just a little nugget of hard pasta still in the center—this is al dente.

5 Ladle about 2 cups of the sauce into a bowl and set it aside as an insurance policy; you want the perfect ratio of pasta to sauce and while you can always add it back, you can't take it out once the pasta is in the pan.

6 Drain the pasta, add it to the pan of sauce, and stir well. Cook the pasta in the sauce, adding more sauce if needed, for another 1 to 2 minutes; the pasta will begin to absorb the sauce and it will cling to the pasta in a lovely little hug. Add the cheese and a drizzle of big fat finishing oil and toss until it's a homogeneous mixture. Divide among serving bowls, top with more Parm, and give each a sprinkle of the crispy critters.

Open your mouth, dive in, and enjoy!

RAVIOLO AL'UOVO
(RICOTTA-NESTLED EGG YOLK)

SERVES: 8 · TIME: ABOUT 30 MINUTES WITH PREMADE PASTA DOUGH

After culinary school, I spent a year in Italy learning to cook Italian food the way the Italians do, the right way. That year was probably one of the most important of my education; I learned a ton from the chefs I worked for—techniques and methods I still rely on every day. I also learned how to make this dish—which is a total showstopper.

Uovo means "egg," and that's what this dish is all about: a lovely golden egg yolk nestled in a bed of creamy ricotta cheese all wrapped up in a tender blanket of pasta. Cut these lovelies open and the yolk flows out of the center. It's an incredibly sophisticated and sexy dish, but deceivingly easy to make—the only catch is you have to cook the raviolis in batches. I realize this may seem like a pain, but it's really the best approach as these ravs are very fragile (and they do cook really quickly, so it's actually not that big a deal). I promise it's worth it, because this recipe will make you a rock star!

MISE EN PLACE

2 cups ricotta cheese

1 cup freshly grated Parmigiano, plus more for garnish

¼ cup chopped fresh Italian parsley

2 large eggs plus 8 large egg yolks

Kosher salt

All-purpose flour, as needed

½ recipe Chef Anne's All-Purpose Pasta Dough (page 102), rolled for ravioli

Semolina flour, as needed

8 tablespoons (1 stick) unsalted butter

2 cups chicken stock (see page 85)

¼ cup chopped fresh sage leaves

1 In a medium bowl, combine the ricotta, Parm, parsley, and 2 whole eggs; mix well and season with salt.

2 Dust a clean work surface lightly with all-purpose flour and lay out two sheets of pasta about 12 inches long; brush them lightly with water. Equally space 4 dollops of the ricotta mixture on each pasta sheet; then use a spoon to make a "nest" or small hole in the center of

each dollop. Carefully separate the remaining eggs (reserve the whites for another purpose) and put a yolk in each ricotta "nest"—the ricotta should lovingly nestle each yolk (if a yolk breaks, scoop it out with a spoon and don't use it).

3 Cover the ricotta nests and egg yolk with another sheet of pasta. Use your index fingers to press around each ricotta nest to seal the edges, then use a fluted ring cutter or dough

roller to cut around each ravioli (they should be 3 to 4 inches in diameter). Reserve the ravioli on a tray generously dusted with semolina.

4   Bring a large pot of well-salted water to a boil. In a large sauté pan, melt half the butter and add half of the chicken stock (you're going to use the remainder for your next batch); season with salt and toss in half the sage. Bring this to a boil (BTB) and reduce to a simmer (RTS).

5   Add 4 of the ravioli to the boiling water and cook for 3 minutes. Using a spider or slotted spoon, carefully transfer the ravioli from the water to the pan with butter and chicken stock and cook for 2 to 3 minutes. If the sauce

reduces too much, add a few drops of the pasta cooking water. The sauce should cling to the ravioli in a buttery hug.

6   Transfer the ravioli to serving plates, spoon a little extra sauce over each one, and finish with a sprinkey-dink of grated Parm. Repeat with the remaining butter, stock, sage, and ravioli.

Molto sexy!

save the leftover egg whites for another purpose. you can even freeze them if you like.

SPAGHETTI
WITH OLIVE-OIL-POACHED TUNA IN TOMATO-FENNEL SAUCE

SERVES: 4 TO 6 · TIME: ABOUT 1¾ HOURS

I used to go to Lupa, Mario Batali's Roman trattoria on Thompson Street in Manhattan, and eat preserved tuna belly with beans. It was SOOOOO good! The tuna belly—which is a highly underrated ingredient—becomes succulent and delicious when it's slow-poached, and that's exactly how I cook it. I use it in a pasta sauce that's full of tomatoes, fennel, and lots of garlic to create a wonderful tomato-y, perfume-y, olive oil-y dish that just screams of Sicily.

One of the great things about tuna belly is that because it's considered the throwaway part of the fish, it's really cheap. You have to spend some time cleaning it, but usually if you pay a bit more you can get it already prepped from your fishmonger (much easier!). If you can't find tuna belly or don't feel like making it, a good substitute is Sicilian tuna packed in olive oil.

MISE EN PLACE

FOR THE TUNA

1 tablespoon fennel seeds
1 pound cleaned tuna belly
Kosher salt
½ teaspoon crushed red pepper
Extra virgin olive oil
2 cloves garlic, smashed

2 bay leaves
1 thyme bundle, tied with butcher's twine

FOR THE SAUCE

Extra virgin olive oil
4 onions, cut into ¼-inch slices
1 fennel bulb, cut into ¼-inch slices, fronds reserved for garnish
Kosher salt

Pinch of crushed red pepper
5 cloves garlic, very thinly sliced
1 28-ounce can San Marzano tomatoes, passed through a food mill
1 tablespoon fennel seeds, toasted and ground (reserved while preparing the tuna)

1 pound spaghetti
Big fat finishing oil

FOR THE TUNA

1 Add the fennel seeds to a small sauté pan and bring to medium-high heat. (You need toasted fennel seeds for both the tuna and the sauce, so toss 2 tablespoons in the pan now and save a step later!) Toast the fennel seeds, shaking the pan frequently, until they are very aromatic and start to turn a brighter shade of green, 3 to 4 minutes. Remove from the heat and grind the seeds in a spice grinder or crush with a mortar and pestle.

2 Season the tuna belly with salt, red pepper, and half the ground fennel seeds (you're saving the other half for the sauce).

3 Preheat the oven to 200°F.

4 Put the tuna in a medium ovenproof saucepan and cover with olive oil. Toss in the garlic, bay leaves, and thyme bundle. Cover and

RECIPE CONTINUES

YOU SAY TOMATO, I SAY SAN MARZANO

San Marzano tomatoes are, as the name suggests, from San Marzano, Italy, outside of Naples. Sweet and delicious, these canned tomatoes are naturally very low in acid. Sometimes you'll notice people add a pinch of sugar to tomatoes when making sauce—this is not to sweeten the sauce so much as to offset the acid in the tomatoes. When you're using San Marzano tomatoes, this isn't necessary because they're naturally super-sweet and low in acid. However, for this same reason, they need a lot of salt to bring out their best flavor . . . accept it and move on.

San Marzano tomatoes are perfect for sauce, *and* they work beautifully with my favorite piece of kitchen equipment: the food mill. It's super-old school but I love using a food mill to purée tomatoes because it lets the seeds slip through, leaving all the big-money stuff up top. Remember, when you put your tomatoes through a food mill, be sure to scrape the pulp off the bottom to get every last bit of tomato-y goodness! This is the stuff that will help thicken the sauce, so you don't want to leave it behind. Got it?

put in the oven; cook for 1 hour. Remove and let cool to room temperature. Use immediately or refrigerate in an airtight container.

FOR THE SAUCE AND PASTA

1 Coat a large wide saucepan with olive oil and add the onions and fennel; season with salt and red pepper and bring to medium heat. Cook the veggies until soft and aromatic, 8 to 10 minutes. Add the garlic and cook for another 2 to 3 minutes.

2 Add the tomatoes, the reserved tablespoon of toasted fennel seeds, and 1 cup water to the pan and season with salt. Bring to a boil (BTB) and reduce to a simmer (RTS); simmer for 30 minutes.

3 Bring a large pot of well-salted water to a boil. Add the pasta and cook for 1 minute less than the instructions on the package suggest. Taste it: It should be toothsome with just a little nugget of hard pasta still in the center—this is al dente.

4 Remove the tuna from the olive oil, break it up, and add it to the sauce.

5 Drain the pasta and add it to the sauce; stir vigorously to combine. Add a drizzle of big fat finishing oil and serve garnished with fennel fronds.

That's no tuna noodle casserole!

TAGLIOLINI
WITH ARUGULA-WALNUT SAUCE

SERVES: 4 TO 6 · TIME: ABOUT 20 MINUTES WITH PREMADE PASTA DOUGH

I LOOOOOVE nuts. And this super-classic preparation, which is hugely flavorful and really easy to make, is all about them. I start by toasting and puréeing walnuts—both of which help bring out their flavor and natural fattiness. Combine them with some sharp cheese and spicy arugula, and you end up with a dish that's luscious and palate cleansing at the same time.

MISE EN PLACE

Kosher salt
1 cup walnuts
3 cups baby arugula

1 clove garlic, smashed
½ cup freshly grated Pecorino
½ cup freshly grated Parmigiano
Extra virgin olive oil

½ cup heavy cream
1 recipe Chef Anne's All-Purpose Pasta Dough (page 102), cut into tagliolini, or 1 pound fresh tagliolini
Big fat finishing oil

1 Preheat the oven to 350°F.

2 Bring a large pot of well-salted water to a boil.

3 Put the walnuts on a baking sheet and roast for 6 to 7 minutes.

4 Combine the walnuts, arugula, garlic, Pecorino, and Parmigiano in a food processor and purée until the mixture is a coarse paste. While the machine is running, drizzle in just enough olive oil to get the paste from coarse to smooth. Stop, scrape down the sides, and add the cream. Pulse, pulse, pulse until the cream is just combined; season with salt and taste to make sure it's delicious.

5 Put the pesto in a large wide saucepan and loosen it with a couple ladlefuls of the pasta water—you don't want it to be thin, but you want it to be a *sauce*. Bring to medium heat.

6 Cook the pasta for 3 to 4 minutes or until tender but still toothsome. Drain the pasta and toss with the sauce, stirring vigorously to coat. Add a drizzle of big fat finishing oil and stir once more. Serve immediately.

I love the feel of nuts in my mouth!

here's a tip: to avoid burning your nuts, set a timer. once you start to smell them— it's too late!

SPAG &
EXCELLENT
"MEATBAWLS"

SERVES: 4 TO 6 · TIME: ABOUT 4 HOURS, MOSTLY UNATTENDED

I LOOOOOVE meatballs—who doesn't? This is my interpretation of the classic Italian-American dish. What makes these meatballs special are two things: First, I cook the onions *before* putting them in the meatball mix. Second, I add water—this helps ensure a moist ball every time!

MISE EN PLACE

FOR THE SAUCE

Extra virgin olive oil

¼ pound pancetta, cut into ¼-inch dice

4 onions, cut into ¼-inch dice

Pinch of crushed red pepper

Kosher salt

4 cloves garlic, smashed and finely chopped

4 28-ounce cans San Marzano tomatoes, passed through a food mill

FOR THE MEATBALLS

Extra virgin olive oil

2 onions, cut into ¼-inch dice

Kosher salt

2 cloves garlic, smashed and chopped

Pinch of crushed red pepper

½ pound ground beef

½ pound ground veal

½ pound ground pork

2 large eggs

1 cup freshly grated Parmigiano, plus more as needed

¼ cup chopped fresh Italian parsley

1 cup bread crumbs

Spaghetti or other pasta

Big fat finishing oil

FOR THE SAUCE

1 Coat a large saucepan with olive oil and add the pancetta; bring to medium heat and cook the pancetta for 6 to 8 minutes. Add the onions and red pepper and season generously with salt; cook until the onions are soft and aromatic, 8 to 10 minutes. Add the garlic and cook for another 2 to 3 minutes, stirring frequently.

2 Add the tomatoes to the pot along with 2 cups of water, adding up to another cup as needed for consistency during the cooking process. Season generously with salt and taste the sauce. Tomatoes need a lot of salt to bring out their best flavor, so don't be shy here. Cook the sauce for 2 to 3 hours, stirring occasionally and tasting frequently. You'll probably need to reseason along the way—that's just how this sauce rolls.

RECIPE CONTINUES

3 Use the sauce right away or let it cool and store in the refrigerator for a few days; it also freezes really well.

FOR THE MEATBALLS

1 Coat a large sauté pan with olive oil, add the onions, and bring to medium-high heat. Season the onions generously with salt and cook until soft and aromatic, 8 to 10 minutes. Add the garlic and red pepper and sauté for another 2 to 3 minutes; turn off the heat and let everything cool.

2 In a large bowl combine the beef, veal, pork, eggs, Parmigiano, parsley, and bread crumbs and season with salt. Using your hands, squish the mixture well to combine. Add the onions and about ½ cup water. Squish, squish, and squish until everything is well combined—the mixture should be quite wet. To check your seasoning, make a 1- to 2-inch tester patty out of the mix; bring a small sauté pan to medium-high heat, add a bit of olive oil, and cook the patty until it's done. Taste it to make sure the seasoning is on the money (it's a travesty to have an underseasoned ball, so don't skip this step!).

3 Preheat the oven to 350°F.

4 Using damp hands, shape the meat into balls, whatever size you like—some people like big balls, some people like small balls. I like them a little bigger than a golf ball. Put the meatballs on a rimmed baking sheet and bake them for about 15 minutes or until they are cooked all the way through. Then, coat a large sauté pan with olive oil and bring to medium-high heat. Brown the meatballs on all sides. If using them right away, toss them in your big pot of sauce with spaghetti, or whatever pasta you like. Drizzle with big fat finishing oil and sprinkle with Parm, toss vigorously, and serve. If you're not using them right away, freeze them on a baking sheet and then toss them in a baggie.

Magnifico meatbawls!

If you have a pot of sauce, you can always pull those meatballs out of the freezer & toss them straight into the sauce - no need to defrost them first!

TAGLIATELLE
WITH BACON, SWEET CORN, BURST CHERRY TOMATOES & ARUGULA

SERVES: 4 TO 6 · TIME: ABOUT 45 MINUTES WITH PREMADE PASTA DOUGH

Where I come from, corn is the epitome of a summer vegetable; we used to drive out to the fields to get ours fresh and just leave our money in a can on the side of the road. So in this dish I combine corn with lovely little cherry tomatoes sautéed until they burst out of excitement, letting their delightful juices flow! Add some bacon and this sauce just steps up, pokes you, and says, "Hi, I'm summer, glad to see you!"

MISE EN PLACE

4 ears of corn, shucked

Extra virgin olive oil

Kosher salt

¼ pound slab bacon, cut into
¼-inch dice

3 cloves garlic, smashed

Pinch of crushed red pepper

1 pint heirloom cherry tomatoes,
assorted colors

1½ cups chicken (see page 85)
or veggie stock

1 recipe Chef Anne's All-Purpose
Pasta Dough (page 102), cut into
tagliatelle, or 1 pound fresh
tagliatelle

1½ cups baby arugula

Big fat finishing oil

½ cup freshly grated Parmigiano

1 Preheat a grill or broiler.

2 Rub the corn with olive oil and sprinkle with salt. Broil or grill the corn until charred on all sides. Cut the kernels off the cob, then run a knife down the cob again to get the remaining sweet bits.

3 Coat a large wide pan with olive oil. Toss in the bacon, garlic, and red pepper; bring to medium-high heat. When the garlic turns golden and is very aromatic, 2 to 3 minutes, remove it from the pan and ditch it—it has fulfilled its garlic destiny. Add the cherry tomatoes to the pan and roll them around until coated. Add 1 cup of the stock, season with salt, reduce the heat to medium, and let the tomatoes cook until they start to burst, 8 to 10 minutes.

4 Bring a large pot of well-salted water to a boil. Add the corn to the pan with tomatoes and bacon and stir to combine; add another ½ cup stock if the liquid level is very low.

5 Drop the pasta in the boiling water and cook for 2 to 3 minutes, or until it's tender but toothsome.

6 Drain the pasta and add it to the veggies along with about ½ cup reserved cooking water; toss vigorously to combine. Remove the pan from the heat, toss in the arugula, drizzle with the big fat finishing oil, and sprinkle with the Parmigiano. Serve immediately.

I love being corny!

TAGLIOLINI
WITH SALSA CRUDA & RICOTTA SALATA

SERVES: 6 TO 8 · TIME: ABOUT 1½ HOURS WITH PREMADE PASTA DOUGH, MOSTLY UNATTENDED

I first encountered this sauce while working in Umbria, and it's one of my favorite summertime pastas. To me, this is Mother Nature's last blast, her crescendo before fall. This is where you take everything she has to give, all those glorious summer ingredients, and toss them together to let the wonderful flavors marry. Then you just barely heat everything up, never actually letting the veggies cook, so they maintain their fresh flavors. Punctuate this with a salty grate of ricotta salata and say, "Mmmmm . . ."

MISE EN PLACE

2 pounds heirloom tomatoes, assorted colors preferably, stemmed, seeded, and cut into ¼-inch dice

1 red onion, cut into ¼-inch dice

1 zucchini, cut into ¼-inch dice

1 bunch of pencil asparagus, cut into ¼-inch rounds

2 cloves garlic, smashed and finely chopped

5 sprigs of fresh oregano, leaves chopped

8 basil leaves, cut into a chiffonade (see page 58)

¼ cup red wine vinegar

Pinch of crushed red pepper

¼ cup extra virgin olive oil

Kosher salt

1 recipe Chef Anne's All-Purpose Pasta Dough (page 102), cut into tagliolini or 1 pound fresh tagliolini

Big fat finishing oil

1 cup coarsely grated ricotta salata (dried salted ricotta cheese)

1 In a large bowl, combine the tomatoes, onion, zucchini, asparagus, garlic, oregano, basil, vinegar, red pepper, and olive oil and season generously with salt; taste to make sure it's delicious and adjust the seasoning if needed. Let the sauce sit for at least 1 hour to allow the flavors to marry.

2 Bring a large pot of well-salted water to a boil.

3 Add two-thirds of the sauce to a large wide pot and bring to medium-high heat—the idea is to heat up the sauce without really cooking it so you maintain the raw integrity of the veggies.

4 Add the pasta to the boiling water and cook until it is tender but still toothsome, 2 to 3 minutes—you don't want any limp noodles. Drain the pasta and add it to the sauce, along with ½ cup reserved pasta cooking water, and stir vigorously. If the pasta needs it, add the reserved sauce (if it's not needed, then you have lunch for tomorrow!). Cook the pasta together with the sauce until the pasta water has evaporated. Give the pasta a drizzle of big fat finishing oil and stir vigorously again. Divide among individual serving dishes and top with the ricotta salata.

Summer in a bowl!

ORECCHIETTE
WITH BROCCOLI RABE PESTO & SAUSAGE

SERVES: 4 TO 6 · TIME: ABOUT 30 MINUTES

When people think pesto, they think basil. But I like to mix pesto up and use broccoli rabe—one of my very favorite vegetables. Broccoli rabe makes a delicious starting point for pesto. Add some sharp cheese and pistachios and you've got an amazing way to transform an old classic. I stick with a traditional combo—bitter rabe and sweet sausage over orecchiette (translated as "little ear")—but I tweak it just enough to make it fresh and fabulous!

MISE EN PLACE

FOR THE PESTO

Kosher salt

2 bunches of broccoli rabe, tough lower stems removed, coarsely chopped into 1-inch lengths

½ cup chopped pistachios

¾ cup freshly grated Parmigiano

Extra virgin olive oil

¼ cup mascarpone

FOR THE PASTA

Extra virgin olive oil

½ pound Italian sausage, sweet or spicy, casings removed

1 pound orecchiette

Big fat finishing oil

Freshly grated Parmigiano

FOR THE PESTO

1 Bring a large pot of well-salted water to a boil. Drop the rabe into the water, give it a swish, and remove it immediately, saving the water to cook your pasta in later.

2 Reserve a cup of the rabe. Toss the rest in a food processor and pulse, pulse, pulse until you have a coarse paste. Add the pistachios and Parm and purée until smooth. If it seems dry, drizzle in a little olive oil while the machine is running. Add the mascarpone and pulse until combined; taste for seasoning. It should be slightly bitter, nutty, and creamy at the same time. Reserve.

FOR THE PASTA

1 Coat a large sauté pan with olive oil and bring to medium-high heat. Add the sausage, using a spoon to break it up, and cook until brown and crumbly, 8 to 10 minutes.

2 Bring your broccoli rabe water back to a boil and toss in the pasta, cooking for 1 minute less than the package recommends. Drain the pasta and add it, along with ½ cup reserved pasta cooking water, the reserved rabe, and two-thirds of the pesto, to the pan with the sausage. Stir to combine and cook until the water evaporates and the pesto is clinging to the pasta. Remove from the heat, drizzle with some big fat finishing oil, sprinkle with more Parm, and stir vigorously to combine. Divide among bowls and serve immediately.

What delightful little ears!

RAVIOLI

WITH FAVA BEANS

SERVES: 4 TO 6 · TIME: ABOUT 1 HOUR WITH PREMADE PASTA DOUGH

Fava beans are one of those things I wait for all year long. When you talk about seasonal cooking, fava beans immediately come to my mind because when they're fresh, there's really nothing like them. I was one of the weird kids who grew up liking lima beans—in fact, I asked for them every birthday dinner (why my mother didn't just serve them to me on a regular basis I'm not really sure). Fava beans to me are a jacked-up version of lima beans, so you can imagine how much I like them. I feature them in this sauce, but then I tuck some sweet pea and cheese action into the ravioli so you get a little pocket of pea-ness on your plate along with those lovely favas!

MISE EN PLACE

Kosher salt

3 cups shelled English peas

2 cups shelled fava beans

2 cups ricotta cheese

1 cup freshly grated Parmigiano, plus more for serving

4 large eggs

All-purpose flour, as needed

1 recipe Chef Anne's All-Purpose Pasta Dough (page 102), rolled for ravioli

Semolina flour, as needed

½ pound (2 sticks) unsalted butter

1 to 1½ cups chicken stock (see page 85)

1 Bring a medium pot of well-salted water to a boil and set up a bowl of well-salted ice water. Drop the peas in the boiling water, let the water return to a boil, and cook the peas for 2 more minutes. Scoop the peas out of the water and plunge them immediately into the ice water. When the peas are cool, remove them from the ice water and reserve. Repeat this process with the fava beans. When the favas are cool, peel off the tough outer layer and reserve the beans.

2 In a food processor, pulse the peas to make a coarse paste. In a large bowl, combine the pea paste, ricotta, Parmigiano, and eggs; mix well, season with salt, and taste to make sure it's delicious.

3 To assemble the ravioli, dust a clean work surface lightly with flour and lay out sheets of pasta about 12 inches long; use a pastry brush to brush the bottom half of the pasta sheets lightly with water. Fill a disposable pastry bag (or a zip-top bag with one corner cut out) with the pea mixture and pipe 1-inch balls of filling onto the pasta about 1½ inches apart. Fold the top half of the pasta sheet over the filling so the top edge meets the bottom edge. Use your index fingers to press around the filling and seal the edges shut. Use a fluted ring cutter or fluted pasta roller to cut out the ravioli; put them on a baking sheet dusted with semolina.

4   Bring a large pot of well-salted water to a boil.

5   Bring a large saucepan to medium heat and add the butter and 1 cup of the chicken stock; season with salt. When the butter has melted, add the fava beans.

6   Add the ravioli to the boiling water and cook for 4 to 5 minutes; scoop out the ravioli and add them to the sauce. Cook the ravioli in the sauce for a couple of minutes, shaking the pan frequently, until the sauce begins to thicken and cling to the pasta. If the sauce seems too thick, add a bit more stock. Put five ravioli on each serving plate, spoon a little extra sauce and some fava beans over each, and sprinkle with Parm to serve.

This is one of my fava-rites!

WHOLE WHEAT PAPPARDELLE

WITH ROASTED BUTTERNUT SQUASH, BROCCOLI RABE & PUMPKIN SEEDS

SERVES: 6 TO 8 · TIME: ABOUT 45 MINUTES WITH PREMADE PASTA DOUGH

This is an amazing dish because it takes everyday ingredients and joins them in a delicious and unexpected collaboration. Both the squash and the broccoli rabe have their own strong personalities—one sweet and one bitter—and each brings something to the party that would be sorely missed if one of them didn't show up. Combined with the nutty, earthy flavor of the whole wheat pasta, this is what I call a real team effort.

MISE EN PLACE

1 butternut squash, peeled and cut into ½-inch dice

Extra virgin olive oil

Kosher salt

1 bunch of broccoli rabe, tough bottom stems removed

3 cloves garlic, smashed

Pinch of crushed red pepper

1½ cups veggie or chicken stock

1 recipe Chef Anne's All-Purpose Pasta Dough (page 102), whole wheat variation (see page 103), cut into pappardelle, or 1 pound fresh pappardelle

1 cup freshly grated Parmigiano

Big fat finishing oil

½ cup pepitas (green pumpkin seeds), toasted

1 Preheat the oven to 375°F.

2 In a large bowl, toss the butternut squash with just enough olive oil to lightly coat it and sprinkle with salt. Put the squash on a baking sheet and roast for about 20 minutes, or until soft. Reserve.

3 Bring a large pot of well-salted water to a boil. Add the broccoli rabe, give it a swish, and immediately remove it from the water; save the water to cook the pasta. When the rabe is cool enough to handle, coarsely chop it and set aside.

4 Coat a large wide saucepan generously with olive oil. Toss in the garlic and red pepper and bring to medium heat. When the garlic is golden brown and very aromatic, 2 to 3 minutes, remove it from the pan and ditch it—it has fulfilled its garlic destiny. Add the roasted squash and the stock to the pan. When the stock has reduced by about half, 5 to 6 minutes, add the broccoli rabe.

5 In the meantime, bring the broccoli rabe water back to a boil, add the pasta, and cook for 4 to 5 minutes or until tender but tooth-

some. Drain the pasta and add it, along with ½ cup reserved pasta cooking water, to the squash and rabe. When the pasta water has evaporated, remove the pan from the heat, add about two-thirds of the Parmigiano, and a big

drizzle of the big fat finishing oil. Toss or stir vigorously to combine. Divide among serving bowls and top with more Parm and the pepitas.

Squash it!

SPINACH & RICOTTA
GNOCCHI
WITH FONTINA FONDUTA

SERVES: 8 TO 10 · TIME: ABOUT 45 MINUTES, NOT INCLUDING OVERNIGHT PREPARATION OF CHEESES

These gnocchi are also called *malfatti* (which translates to "badly made") or *gnudi* (which means "nude") because essentially these are ravioli without the pasta—they're naked! No matter what you call them, I ADORE these delicate little cheese dumplings. They're little bundles of spinach and ricotta sitting on top of melted Fontina mixed with heavy cream, mascarpone, and egg yolks. A little bit of this dish goes a long way—right to my booty usually!

MISE EN PLACE

FOR THE GNOCCHI

2 pounds ricotta cheese

1 10-ounce package frozen spinach, defrosted, water squeezed out, and finely chopped

4 large eggs

2 cups freshly grated Parmigiano, plus more for sprinkling

2 or 3 grates of fresh nutmeg

Kosher salt

¼ to ½ cup all-purpose flour, plus more as needed

Semolina flour, as needed

FOR THE FONDUTA

1 pound Fontina cheese, cut into 1-inch squares

2 cups heavy cream

1 cup mascarpone

6 large egg yolks

ANNE ALERT!

You need to prepare the cheeses for this delicious dish overnight—so plan ahead!

FOR THE GNOCCHI

1 Wrap the ricotta in two layers of cheesecloth, secure with string, and put it in a colander set over a bowl in the fridge to drain overnight; the ricotta needs to be really dry.

2 Unwrap the ricotta—the texture should be pretty dry and crumbly—and pass it through a food mill using the attachment with the biggest holes. In a large bowl, combine the ricotta, spinach, eggs, Parmigiano, and nutmeg and mix well; taste and season with salt if needed. Add ¼ cup all-purpose flour to the bowl and stir. If the mixture is still very wet, add the remaining flour—you want this to be firm enough to hold its own shape.

3 Dust a baking sheet generously with all-purpose flour. Coat another baking sheet generously with semolina. Fill a disposable pastry bag (or a zip-top bag with one corner cut out) with the ricotta mixture and pipe 1-inch balls onto the flour-lined tray. Shake the tray around to coat the balls in flour, then gently roll each ball around in your hand to smooth it. Put the gnocchi on the semolina-lined tray until you're ready to cook.

FOR THE FONDUTA

1 In a large bowl, combine the Fontina and cream, cover, and refrigerate overnight.

2 Fill a small saucepan with 1 inch of water and bring to a boil (BTB), then reduce to a simmer (RTS). Put the Fontina and cream in a large heatproof bowl that will sit comfortably on the saucepan without touching the water (a double boiler setup). Whisk the cream frequently until the cheese has melted; then stir in the mascarpone. Beat in the egg yolks one at a time and cook until the mixture has thickened and is hot. Turn off the heat, cover the fonduta with plastic wrap, and reserve in a warm spot.

TO ASSEMBLE THE DISH

1 Bring a large pot of well-salted water to a boil. Reduce the heat until the water just simmers and carefully add the gnocchi to the water; cook the dumplings until they float and begin to swell.

2 While the gnocchi cook, spoon the fonduta onto individual serving plates, using the back of a spoon to spread it into 4- to 5-inch circles. Using a spider or slotted spoon, carefully remove the gnocchi from the cooking water, blot them on a tea towel (you don't want to make your lovely sauce watery), and arrange five gnocchi on each plate in the sauce. Sprinkle with Parm and serve.

It's so easy being cheeeeeesy!

RISOTTO-
WITHOUT-A-RECIPE

SERVES: 4 TO 6 · TIME: ABOUT 45 MINUTES

If you wheel your grocery cart down the rice aisle, you will not find "risotto." Risotto is not a type of rice—it's a method used for cooking Arborio or Carnaroli rice. And once you learn how to make risotto using my Risotto-Without-a-Recipe method, you'll be able to make any kind of risotto simply by adding ingredients and flavorings to this basic technique.

MISE EN PLACE

Extra virgin olive oil

2 onions, cut into ¼-inch dice

Kosher salt

6 to 7 cups chicken stock
(see page 85)

2 cups Arborio or Carnaroli rice

2 cups dry white wine

2 cups dry white wine ½ to ¾ cup
freshly grated Parmigiano

2 tablespoons unsalted butter

1 Coat a large saucepan generously with olive oil and add the onions; season with salt and bring the pan to medium-high heat. Cook the onions, stirring frequently, until soft and aromatic, 8 to 10 minutes.

2 Heat the stock in a medium saucepan and keep warm.

3 Add the rice to the onions and stir; toast the rice for 2 to 3 minutes, stirring frequently. The rice should stick a little bit (not a lot) to the bottom of the pan.

4 Add enough of the wine to cover the surface of the rice and cook, stirring frequently, for 3 to 4 minutes or until the rice absorbs the wine.

5 When all the wine has been absorbed, add enough of the hot chicken stock to cover the rice. Season with salt and taste the liquid; it should taste good. Stir frequently until all the stock has been absorbed; repeat this process twice more (for a total of three additions).

6 When the last addition of the stock has been absorbed, taste a couple of grains; the rice should feel cooked but still have a little bite to it, and it should look loose and creamy (add another ladle or two of stock if the rice has tightened up).

7 Remove the pan from the heat and add the Parm and butter, whipping the risotto vigorously until well combined. Brace yourself and really whip the hell out of the rice—the Italian word for this is *mantecare,* and this is the step the Italians don't tell you about! This sets the beautiful texture of your risotto, making it tight and creamy at the same time. Serve immediately.

Risott-ooohhh!!!!

RISOTTO
WITH ROCK SHRIMP, LEMON & HERBS

SERVES: 4 TO 6 · TIME: ABOUT 45 MINUTES

When you use my Risotto-Without-a-Recipe technique (opposite), you can flavor it with anything you like. Sweet little rock shrimp, bright lemon, and fresh herbs are one of my favorite combos.

MISE EN PLACE

Extra virgin olive oil
2 onions, cut into ¼-inch dice
Kosher salt
6 to 7 cups chicken stock
(see page 85)

2 cups Arborio or Carnaroli rice
2 cups dry white wine
Juice and grated zest of 2 lemons
1½ pounds rock shrimp, rinsed and picked through for any shells

½ to ¾ cup freshly grated Parmigiano
2 tablespoons unsalted butter
1 bunch of fresh chives, finely chopped
1 bunch of fresh oregano, leaves finely chopped

1 Coat a large saucepan generously with olive oil and add the onions; season with salt and bring to medium-high heat. Cook the onions, stirring frequently, until soft and aromatic, 8 to 10 minutes.

2 Heat the stock in a medium saucepan and keep warm.

3 Add the rice to the onions and stir; toast the rice for 2 to 3 minutes, stirring frequently. The rice should stick a little bit (not a lot) to the bottom of the pan.

4 Add enough of the wine to cover the surface of the rice and cook, stirring frequently, for 3 to 4 minutes or until the rice absorbs the wine.

5 When all the wine has been absorbed, add enough of the hot chicken stock to cover the rice. Season with salt and taste the liquid; it should taste good. Stir frequently until all the stock has been absorbed; repeat this process, adding more hot stock to cover the rice and stirring until absorbed.

6 Add the final batch of chicken stock (for a total of three additions) along with the lemon juice and zest; stir. When the stock has absorbed about halfway, add the shrimp and stir continuously.

7 When the last addition of the stock has been absorbed, taste a couple of grains; the rice should feel cooked but still have a little bite to it, and it should look loose and creamy (add another ladle or two of stock if the rice has tightened up). The shrimp should be pink and plump.

8 Remove the pan from the heat and add the Parm, butter, chives, and oregano, whipping the risotto vigorously until well combined—then serve.

Rockin' risotto!

FARROTTO
WITH LOBSTER, PEAS, MINT & OREGANO

SERVES: 4 TO 6 · TIME: ABOUT 1½ HOURS

Farro is an ancient grain that's used in traditional Tuscan and Umbrian cooking—kind of like a cross between barley and wheat berries. I love making farro in the style of risotto—a.k.a. farrotto. By using my Risotto-Without-a-Recipe technique (page 136) and substituting farro for rice, you end up with something rich and chewy and nutty all at the same time. Like risotto, farrotto is a blank canvas for whatever you're feeling passionate about. Whatever ingredients are in season, whatever flavors you're in the mood for, whatever's freshest. Whenever I cook for big events and have to feed a lot of people, I always make farrotto because it's quick, it doesn't cost a lot, and it's a huge crowd pleaser. It's a win-win-win.

MISE EN PLACE

FOR THE LOBSTERS
Extra virgin olive oil
1 onion, coarsely chopped
2 celery ribs, coarsely chopped
2 carrots, coarsely chopped
3 cloves garlic, smashed
1 lemon, cut in half

1 thyme bundle, tied with butcher's twine
Kosher salt
2 1¼- to 1½-pound lobsters

FOR THE FARRO
Extra virgin olive oil
1 onion, cut into ¼-inch dice
Kosher salt
2 cups semipearled farro

2 cups white wine
Lobster stock, as needed (reserved from cooking the lobsters)
2 cups shelled English peas
3 sprigs of fresh mint, leaves cut into a chiffonade (see page 58)
3 sprigs of fresh oregano, leaves chopped
2 tablespoons unsalted butter
⅓ cup freshly grated Parmigiano

FOR THE LOBSTERS

1 Coat a large tall pot with olive oil, toss in the onion, celery, and carrots, and bring to medium-high heat. Cook until the veggies are soft and aromatic, 8 to 10 minutes. Add the garlic and cook for another 2 to 3 minutes. Fill the pot with water and toss in the lemon halves and the thyme bundle; season lightly with salt. Bring the pot to a boil (BTB) and add the lobsters; cover and cook for 12 minutes.

2 Use tongs to remove the lobsters from the pot and set them aside (save the cooking water!). When the lobsters are cool enough to handle, remove the meat from the shells and add the shells back to the lobster pot; simmer for 30 minutes. Strain the shells and veggies from the cooking liquid. Voilà—you've made lobster stock! If you're using this right away, keep it hot. If not, freeze it.

3 Cut the lobster meat into bite-size pieces and reserve.

FOR THE FARROTTO

1 Coat a large wide pot generously with olive oil, add the onion, and season with salt. Bring the pan to medium-high heat and cook the onion until soft and aromatic, 8 to 10 minutes.

2 Add the farro and cook, stirring frequently, for 5 minutes. Add the wine; it should cover the surface of the farro. Continue to cook, stirring frequently, until the wine is totally absorbed, 5 to 7 minutes.

3 Add enough hot lobster stock to the pan to cover the surface of the farro; stir to combine. Taste for seasoning and adjust if needed. Cook, stirring frequently, until the lobster stock is absorbed, repeat this process two more times, then add the peas.

4 After the last addition of stock has been absorbed, taste the farro. If it's firm or dry, add a little more stock and cook a little longer.

5 When the farro is tender, add the lobster meat, mint, oregano, butter, and Parm and stir vigorously. REALLY WHIP IT! This will set the perfect texture of the farro. Taste to make sure it's delicious and serve.

Farrotto—it's FAR out!

KILLER
MAC & CHEESE
WITH BACON

SERVES: 6 TO 8 · TIME: ABOUT 50 MINUTES

Everyone thinks of mac and cheese as comfort food, but there's a lot of bad mac and cheese out there, and frankly, that food makes me UNcomfortable! Great mac and cheese should be creamy and tangy and luscious—it should get me excited with every bite. I promise that this recipe is what mac and cheese should be. And it's got bacon! What could be better?

MISE EN PLACE

Extra virgin olive oil

6 slices bacon, cut crosswise into ½-inch strips

3 tablespoons unsalted butter

1 onion, cut into ¼-inch dice

Kosher salt

½ cup all-purpose flour

1 quart whole milk, plus more as needed

1 pound shells or other short pasta

2 cups freshly grated Cheddar cheese

2 cups freshly grated Fontina cheese

1 cup freshly grated Parmigiano

¼ cup Dijon mustard

Tabasco or other hot sauce, to taste

1 Drizzle a bit of olive oil in a large saucepan, add the bacon, and bring the pan to medium heat; stir the bacon occasionally. When it's brown and crispy, 6 to 8 minutes, remove it from the pan, drain on paper towels, and reserve that deliciousness. Do not discard the bacon fat!

2 Add the butter and onion to the pan with the fat, season with salt, and cook until the onion is soft and aromatic, 8 to 10 minutes. Add the flour and cook, stirring frequently, for 4 to 5 minutes or until the mixture looks like wet sand. Slowly whisk in the milk, season with salt, bring to a boil (BTB), and reduce to a simmer (RTS); cook over low heat for 8 to 10 minutes more or until the mixture is slightly thicker than heavy cream.

3 In the meanwhile, bring a large pot of well-salted water to a boil. Add the pasta to the boiling water and cook for 1 minute less than the instructions on the package suggest. Taste it: It should be toothsome with just a little nugget of hard pasta still in the center—this is al dente. Drain the pasta and reserve.

4 Add the Cheddar, Fontina, and Parmigiano to the milk mixture and whisk to combine. Add the mustard and a few shakes of Tabasco; taste and adjust the seasoning if needed, adding a little more milk if the mixture seems too thick. Stir in the cooked bacon and pasta. The mixture should be very creamy and flavorful. Serve immediately or transfer to a baking dish or ramekins and reheat in a 375°F. oven.

Now that's killer!

CH NO. 4

SECONDS

{ the main event }

The thing about seconds, or main courses, is that often by the time I get around to eating them, I've had too many appetizers and too much wine and I'm just not that hungry anymore. I guess sometimes I should just start with seconds because I do love them—after all, they're the main event!

AS A CHEF, I FIND THAT SECONDS CHALLENGE ME

creatively in a way that piccolini or firsts don't. Because they feature a larger portion of protein, I'm always trying to think of unique and interesting ways to make a steak or a piece of chicken exciting. Getting creative with a bigger hunk of protein requires skill and thoughtfulness; you have to use your imagination and a variety of different cooking techniques to make the main event new, enticing, and seductive over and over again.

In my experience, knowing how to add flavor while maintaining the integrity of the protein is essential for a great main course. I'm not much of a sauce girl, so for me, adding flavor means relying on marinating, dry rubbing, and beautiful brining! I'm always thinking: How can I use the skills I have as a chef to take what's freshest and make it taste fabulous and new at the same time?

That's why, in addition to cooking skills (which I'll share with you), seasonality is the key to making special main courses. Using the best ingredients available—what's in season—to showcase a piece of meat or fish can take a good main course and turn it into a showstopper.

For me, every season is like an old friend coming back to visit. What I do with a pork chop in the wintertime is not the same as what I do with it in the spring. Not only do my techniques change, but my ingredients change too. In the summer I'm more inclined to grill or sauté and serve the main course with produce fresh out of the garden, ingredients at their peak of perfection. When it's hot out I want to enjoy the weather! I want to get

outside, put some Prosecco or beer on ice, throw some lovely fish and glorious veggies on the fire, and just let Mother Nature's bounty shine as simply as possible.

Fall is totally different. It's one of my favorite seasons because everyone is back from being scattered during summer vacation. It's a time to reconnect with friends, to enjoy festivals and community activities, to go apple picking or hit the pumpkin patch. Fall is sweater weather—when the air just starts to get cool and crisp. The tomato season is over, but the big harvest is in, the market is super-bountiful, and there's tons of produce to play with. It's exciting for me to make the most of what's fresh and available before we all hunker down for the cold weather.

When winter arrives, my approach changes again. I want to stay home and curl up on the couch with a big glass of red wine. I want to spend time with friends and family and enjoy the beautiful smell of short ribs or lamb shanks braising or root vegetables roasting in the oven. Winter is when I crave hearty meals and turn my attention to stews and big meaty main courses.

Then, after hibernating for a few months, I'm always excited for spring—it's like the world is waking up, rubbing its eyes and saying, "Good morning!" I crave fresh, lovely produce after months of root vegetables and am always totally psyched for the first fresh peas and asparagus. But no matter what the season, I look for the ingredients that scream, "Cook me now!" and I let them tell me what recipes will make the most out of dinner's main event.

Grilled Chicken with Lemons & Dijon

Rosemary & Lemon Roasted Chicken with Gravy

Braised Chicken Thighs with Mushrooms & Almond Purée

Duck Breast with Dried Fruit & Vin Santo

Chef Anne's Cheater's Duck Confit & Bitter Greens

Dry Rubbed Bone-In Rib Eye (Just Good Stuff)

Big Brown Braised Short Ribs with Horseradish

Pork Milanese & Escarole Salad with Pickled Red Onions,
Hazelnuts & Pecorino

Polpetti Burgers

Rockin' Porchetta with Fall Veggies

Braised Cabbage Stuffed with Sausage & Fennel

Brined Pork Chops with Fennel Pollen

Rack of Lamb Crusted with Black Olives

Braised Lamb Shanks

Whole Braised Veal Shanks

Seared Red Snapper with Sicilian Cauliflower
& Parsley Salad

Seared Crispy-Skin Black Bass

Halibut in Paper with Yummy Summer Veg

Whole Roasted Fish with Sliced Potatoes,
Olives & Herbs

GRILLED CHICKEN
WITH LEMONS & DIJON

SERVES: 4 · TIME: ABOUT 2½ HOURS, MOSTLY UNATTENDED

Grilled chicken is totally ubiquitous—it's on every menu and it's usually no big whoop. In fact, it's often totally boring. But this grilled chicken is SOOOOO worth getting excited about! It's slathered in mustard, lemon, rosemary, and spicy crushed red pepper so it just titillates your palate with flavor. Then it's grilled until the outside is tangy, crusty, and crispy while the inside stays nice and moist. To make this as super-sexy as possible, it's served with a perfectly charred and caramelized lemon half for an extra squeeze of flavor.

MISE EN PLACE

4 lemons, 2 zested and juiced, 2 halved

1 cup Dijon mustard

2 tablespoons finely chopped fresh rosemary

1 teaspoon crushed red pepper

2 cloves garlic, smashed and finely chopped

Kosher salt

Extra virgin olive oil

2 3-pound chickens, backbone removed, and split in half

1 In a small bowl, combine the lemon zest, juice, mustard, rosemary, red pepper, garlic, and a pinch of salt. Add 1 to 2 tablespoons of olive oil to the mustard mixture to loosen it slightly. Slather this mixture generously all over the chickens and let them hang out for up to 2 hours at room temperature or overnight in the fridge. (If any of the mustard mixture is left over, save it for reslathering while the chicken is cooking.)

2 Preheat the grill to medium (you want the chicken to cook on the grill as long as possible without burning to develop lovely crispy, tasty, tangy skin). Place the chicken on the grill skin side down and cook for 5 to 6 minutes. If the

chicken flares up, move it to a cooler part of the grill; you don't want sooty film on the chicken (it won't taste good).

3 Once the chicken has started to brown and crisp, it's a good idea to close the grill to allow the heat to cook the chicken from all directions. You want to cook the chicken skin side down for a total of 10 to 12 minutes, then turn it over and cook it for another 10 to 12 minutes. If you're using a grill pan, you can transfer the chicken to a 375°F. oven when it's ready to flip so it can finish cooking. If there is leftover mustard mixture, use it to paint the skin of the chicken on the second side. The chicken is done when an instant-read thermometer registers 165°F.

4 When the chicken is nearly done, place the lemon halves on the grill cut side down and leave them alone until brown and caramelized, 5 to 6 minutes. (These will smell great while they're grilling!)

5 Remove the chicken from the heat and serve with the grilled lemon for extra lemony goodness.

That's what I call a tangy chick!

ROASTED
CHICKEN
WITH GRAVY

SERVES: 4 TO 6 · TIME: ABOUT 2½ HOURS, MOSTLY UNATTENDED

Even the simplest roasted chicken always seems like a special dinner to me. I'm not sure why; maybe it's because making a whole bird is like having a mini-Thanksgiving. The irony, of course, is that Thanksgiving is a huge deal and a ton of work, while there are few dinners faster or easier than roast chicken. All you have to do is buy a nice bird, lube it up, shoot it in the oven, and voilà! You have a beautiful chicken dinner. Add some gravy to that and mmmmm . . . Just for the record, I'm not a gravy strainer, but if you are, knock yourself out!

MISE EN PLACE

3 sprigs of fresh rosemary, leaves finely chopped

Pinch of crushed red pepper

2 lemons, zested and juiced

4 cloves garlic, 2 smashed and finely chopped, 2 just smashed

Kosher salt

Extra virgin olive oil

1 4½- to 5-pound chicken

2 onions, cut into ½-inch dice

2 celery ribs, cut into ½-inch dice

2 carrots, cut into ½-inch dice

1 quart chicken stock (see page 85)

¼ cup all-purpose flour

½ cup dry white wine

1 Preheat the oven to 450°F.

2 In a small bowl, combine the rosemary, red pepper, lemon zest and juice, and chopped garlic; season generously with salt and drizzle in just enough olive oil to make a paste.

3 Using your fingers, gently work your way under the skin of the chicken to separate it from the breast and the leg meat, then massage half of the herb paste under the skin. Rub the remaining paste all over the outside of the bird; really lube it up so that the paste acts like suntan oil and the skin gets nice and brown and crispy (the bird will also be really well seasoned!).

4 Truss the chicken (see opposite).

5 Put the smashed garlic, onions, celery, and carrots in the bottom of a roasting pan. Add 1 cup of the chicken stock and a sprinkle of salt, then plunk the chicken on top, breast side up (the soft side, breasts are soft!), and put the pan in the oven.

6 Cook for 20 minutes, then check the bird. When it's brown and lovely on top, pull it out of the oven and use tongs to turn it over in a little chicken pirouette. Cook for another 20 minutes.

TRUST ME! TRUSSING WILL CHANGE YOUR LIFE

Your chicken will never taste the same again—I promise! Trussing helps keep your chicken in that lovely football shape (once you get the hang of it, your chickens will look as perfect as that turkey in the Norman Rockwell painting). It also evens out the cooking process; by bringing the legs up to protect the breast, trussing helps keep the white meat juicy and allows the heat to hit the legs more evenly.

Don't be scared, trussing is super-simple: Take about 30 inches of butcher's twine (don't bother to measure; just cut off a nice long piece) and, with the legs pointing away from you, center the string under the legs. Pull the legs gently back toward you and make an X with the string. Drop the cross of the X away from you and between the legs, pulling it tightly to create loops or "handcuffs" around each leg. Then pull the loops tightly around the chicken. Pull the string back toward you and around the back of the chicken, then tie it in a bow or a knot, whatever. Look at you, all trussed up and ready to go!

7 Reduce the heat to 375°F. and turn the chicken over again. Spoon some of the pan juices over the chicken every 15 minutes or so. Keep an eye on the vegetables—move them around now and then, and if they start to brown too much, add a little more stock, about ½ cup at a time. Cook for another 45 minutes.

8 Remove the chicken from the oven and insert an instant-read thermometer into the crease between the breast and thigh; it should read 160°F. If not, continue cooking until it does. Remove the chicken from the roasting pan, cover with foil, and let rest for 15 to 20 minutes.

9 Use a spoon to skim and discard as much of the excess fat as you can from the vegetables in the roasting pan by propping up one side of the pan a bit so all the liquid runs to one end; you won't get all of it, but that's okay—fat tastes good! Put the roasting pan on the stovetop over medium heat. Sprinkle the flour over the veg

and whisk; the mixture will turn to a paste, which is what you want. Slowly add the wine and continue whisking until most of the lumps have dissolved and the wine has reduced by half, 3 to 4 minutes. Add the remaining stock, bring to a boil (BTB), and reduce to a simmer (RTS); cook for 8 to 10 minutes, or until the gravy thickens. Taste and season with salt as needed.

10 To carve the chicken, pull the leg and thigh away from the breast until the thighbone pops out of the socket (a sign that the chicken is cooked properly). Use a carving knife to separate the thigh and drumstick at the connecting joint. To remove the breast meat, feel for the ridge of the breastbone in the center of the chicken and carefully slice down around the ribcage on both sides. Serve with the gravy.

Tastes like chicken!

BRAISED
CHICKEN
THIGHS
WITH MUSHROOMS & ALMOND PURÉE

SERVES: 4 · TIME: ABOUT 1½ HOURS

I LOOOOOVE dark meat chicken! Especially chicken thighs—they're succulent and delicious, the perfect portion size (two thighs per person), and they're cheap. I also love nuts. In this recipe I put these two ingredients together and take the humble chicken thigh to a totally new level. I braise these lovelies with lots of mushrooms and then thicken the sauce with toasted almond purée. The result is a dish that is surprisingly rich and, thanks to the nuts, has an excellent mouthfeel. It's definitely one of the best recipes I've ever come up with.

MISE EN PLACE

Extra virgin olive oil

8 chicken thighs

Kosher salt

2 onions, cut into ¼-inch dice

Pinch of crushed red pepper

2 cloves garlic, smashed and finely chopped

2 pounds assorted mushrooms (shiitake, oyster, or cremini are all great), trimmed, cleaned, and sliced

1 cup dry white wine

4 to 6 cups chicken stock (see page 85)

1 thyme bundle, tied with butcher's twine

2 bay leaves

½ cup whole blanched almonds, toasted

Chopped fresh chives, for garnish

1 Coat a large, wide, straight-sided pan with olive oil and bring to high heat. Season the chicken generously with salt and add it, skin side down, to the pan—you should hear a big sizzle. If you don't, remove the chicken and wait. When you put chicken in a hot pan, the first thing it wants to do is stick there and the first thing you want to do is move it. Resist the urge. It will unstick itself when it's ready. When the skin is brown and crispy, 5 to 7 minutes, turn the chicken over and brown the other side. Remove the chicken from the pan and reserve.

2 Ditch the fat and lower the heat. Add another splash of olive oil to the pan and add the onions. Season with salt and red pepper and cook over medium heat for 8 to 10 minutes or until the onions are soft and aromatic; then add the garlic and cook for another 2 to 3 minutes, stirring frequently.

3 Add the mushrooms, season with salt, and cook for 4 to 5 minutes or until soft and aromatic. Add the wine and cook until reduced by half, 3 to 4 minutes.

4 Return the chicken to the pan, pour in enough stock to almost cover the chicken, and add the thyme bundle and bay leaves. Bring to a boil (BTB), reduce to a simmer (RTS), and cook for 30 minutes. Add a little more stock if the liquid level gets low.

5 While the chicken cooks, purée the almonds in a food processor. Once they are ground, drizzle in a little olive oil while the machine is running to make a loose paste. Season with salt and reserve.

6 When the chicken has simmered for 30 minutes, remove it from the pan and reserve; remove the bay leaves and thyme bundle and discard. Stir the almond purée into the sauce and taste for seasoning, adding more salt if needed. Bring to a boil (BTB) and reduce to a simmer (RTS) to thicken the sauce if needed. Serve the chicken draped with the sauce and garnished with chives.

Now that's nutty *and* saucy!

DUCK BREAST

WITH DRIED FRUIT & VIN SANTO

SERVES: 4 · TIME: ABOUT 45 MINUTES

Duck is one of those dishes that can be intimidating because it seems fancy and elegant. But there's nothing to be scared of—making great duck just takes patience. To get a really beautiful, crackling, brown piece of skin you have to take your time and render the fat SLOWLY. If you rush it, you'll end up with crispy skin but a thick layer of fat between the skin and the meat— which is totally icky. Taking your time to render the fat will not only make your duck absolutely delicious, but it will also leave you with a treasure trove of duck fat—an ingredient that in restaurant kitchens is considered liquid gold and makes killer Crispy Crunchy Duck Fat Potatoes (page 219).

I think that duck lends itself to sweet flavors, so in this dish I use a sweet Tuscan wine—Vin Santo—to reconstitute dried fruit to make a chutney-like sauce with rich chicken stock. Together the rich, meaty, succulent duck and the intense, fruity sauce make this dish perfect for a holiday, a special occasion, or even a Tuesday.

MISE EN PLACE

½ cup dried apricots, cut into quarters

½ cup dried apples, cut into ½-inch chunks

½ cup dried cherries

1 cup Vin Santo

4 small or 2 large duck breasts

Kosher salt

Extra virgin olive oil

1 cup chicken stock (see page 85)

Leaves from 5 or 6 sprigs of fresh thyme

1 In a small bowl, soak the apricots, apples, and cherries in the Vin Santo.

2 Using a knife, cut or score the fat of the duck breasts in a crosshatched pattern, cutting through the fat, down to the meat, but not into the meat (this allows the fat to escape more easily as it cooks). Season generously with salt.

3 Preheat the oven to 350°F.

4 Coat a large sauté pan with about a tablespoon of olive oil. Place the duck breasts skin side down in the pan (be sure that the duck fits in the pan comfortably and is not crowded). Bring the pan to low heat and render the fat from the duck breasts. This needs to be done S-L-O-W-L-Y; otherwise the fat will be sealed into the skin and will not render out. This process will take about 20 to 25 minutes, maybe more. As the fat builds up in the pan, scoop it out, but SAVE IT!

5 When the fat has rendered from the breasts you will see the meat through the score marks. At this point, crank up the heat and brown both

sides of the duck, 2 to 3 minutes per side. Then move the duck to a rimmed baking sheet and place it in the preheated oven for 5 to 6 minutes for medium-rare. Remove any remaining fat from the pan and set the pan aside to make the sauce (look at me—saving you dishes!). Remove the duck from the oven and let rest for about 10 minutes before slicing.

6 Strain the Vin Santo from the dried fruit, add it to the sauté pan, bring to medium-high heat, and reduce it until it's almost a syrup. Add ½ cup of the chicken stock, all the dried fruit,

and the thyme leaves to the pan; season with salt. When the chicken stock has reduced and the sauce looks kind of chunky, add the remaining chicken stock; bring to a boil (BTB), cook for 2 to 3 minutes, and turn off the heat. Taste to make sure the sauce is yummy and reseason if needed.

7 Slice each duck breast on the bias, fan the meat on a plate, and spoon some of the sauce on and around the duck.

What fabulous fowl!

CHEATER'S
DUCK CONFIT
& BITTER GREENS

SERVES: 6 · TIME: ABOUT 2½ HOURS

When I worked at Savoy in SoHo, we had salt-roasted duck on the menu but we served only the breasts, so there was always an excess of duck legs hanging around. We'd eat the legs at our family meal, but after a while everyone was sick of them. Then one night, I was in a pinch for an hors d'oeuvres idea, and that's when I came up with my cheater's confit. As they say, desperation can be inspiration!

My confit tastes just as good and authentic as a traditional confit, but it's SOOOOO much faster. As far as I'm concerned, the time you save with my recipe is outstanding (this is one streamlined operation!) and so is the flavor.

MISE EN PLACE

6 duck legs
Kosher salt
Extra virgin olive oil

6 onions, thinly sliced
1 bottle of dry white wine
1 thyme bundle, tied with butcher's twine

8 bay leaves
1 bunch of dandelion greens, washed, dried, tough lower stems removed, and cut into 1-inch lengths
Red wine vinegar

1 Season the duck legs generously with salt. Coat a roasting pan lightly with olive oil and lay the duck legs skin side down in a single layer. Put the pan on the stove and bring to medium heat. Cook the legs until the fat slowly begins to melt. This will take 20 to 30 minutes and you don't want to rush it—this part of the process is worth the effort! When a decent amount of fat has been rendered, about ½ inch, raise the heat and brown the legs on both sides. Once browned, remove them from the pan and reserve. Yum! Doesn't this smell good?

2 Preheat the oven to 400°F.

3 Add the onions to the fat in the pan, season generously with salt, and stir to coat; cook over medium heat for 30 minutes, stirring occasionally. Taste to make sure they're well seasoned and add salt if needed.

4 Return the duck legs to the pan and snuggle them in with all the onions. Add the wine, thyme bundle, and bay leaves and cover the pan with foil.

GETTING COMFY WITH CONFIT!

Confit is a classic way of preserving food, most commonly used with duck. It's when you cook something in its own fat and then store it in the fat. Confit is SOOOOO good! It's luscious and rustic; think of it as fancy comfort food.

To make traditional confit you cure the meat overnight with salt and shallots, cook it to render the fat, and then store it in its own fat.

To make my "cheater's" confit, you render the duck fat low and slow—don't rush it! You want to melt as much fat off of the duck legs as possible. Then you caramelize lots of onions in the duck fat, toss in a bunch of white wine, thyme, and bay leaves, and braise the duck with the onions and the fat. It's hugely flavorful and a lot faster than classic confit.

5 Put the pan in the oven and cook for about 1½ hours, stirring every 30 minutes or so to be sure the onions aren't burning. When the duck is done it should be incredibly flavorful, tender, and almost falling off the bone.

6 In a large bowl, combine the greens with some red wine vinegar, a bit of salt, a nice drizzle of the warm duck fat from the pan, and some of the caramelized onions. To serve, place a large mound of the dressed dandelion greens on a plate, lay a duck leg on the greens, and top with a few more onions.

That's just ducky!!!

If you have any lovely duck fat left over, you'll want to use it to make my killer crispy crunchy duck fat potatoes (page 219).

BONE-IN RIB EYE

(JUST GOOD STUFF)

SERVES: 4 · TIME: ABOUT 20 MINUTES ACTIVE TIME AFTER 24 HOURS IN THE RUB

Rib eye is my favorite cut of steak, especially when it's on the bone. It's big and fatty and luscious. And when you add a dry rub, it goes from delicious to delicious-PLUS. Enough said.

MISE EN PLACE

2 tablespoons kosher salt

2 tablespoons packed light or dark brown sugar

1 teaspoon crushed red pepper, ground

2 teaspoons pimentón (smoked paprika)

1 teaspoon garlic powder

2 teaspoons cumin seeds, toasted and ground (see page 17)

2 22- to 24-ounce bone-in rib eye steaks

Big fat finishing oil

ANNE ALERT!

I like to give this steak twenty-four hours to really absorb the lovely flavors of the rub, but if you're in a hurry, even a couple hours will do.

1 In a small bowl, combine the salt, brown sugar, red pepper, pimentón, garlic powder, and cumin. Rub the outside of each steak generously and evenly with the rub (if there's leftover rub, save it for your next steak). Wrap each rubbed steak in plastic and refrigerate for at least 24 hours.

2 Preheat a grill.

3 Remove the steaks from the fridge 20 to 30 minutes before you're ready to cook to allow them to come to room temperature. Remove the plastic wrap.

4 Place the steaks on the grill and char them well over medium-high heat, 3 to 4 minutes per side, until they're really nicely browned. Move the steaks to a cooler part of the grill and continue cooking for another 3 to 4 minutes per side for medium rare. Remove the steaks from the grill and let them rest somewhere warm for 8 to 10 minutes.

5 Cut the meat off the bone and slice it on the bias across the grain. Arrange the sliced steak and the bone on a serving plate and drizzle with big fat finishing oil to serve.

I wanna STEAK in that!

BIG BROWN BRAISED
SHORT RIBS
WITH HORSERADISH

SERVES: 6 TO 8 · TIME: ABOUT 3½ HOURS

Historically, short ribs have been a throwaway piece of meat. But in the restaurant business, part of the job is figuring out how to make the most of every ingredient—which means turning a cheap cut of meat into a super-special meal. However, the secret to braising is out, which means short ribs are no longer an inexpensive cut. Still, with my big brown braising technique, they are totally amazing and well worth splurging on.

Be sure to cook these LOW and SLOW—that's the secret. Take your time getting these lovelies nice and brown, then shoot them in the oven and treat them like a stepchild. Just forget about 'em until they're tender and crazy delicious!

MISE EN PLACE

6 to 8 bone-in short ribs

Kosher salt

Extra virgin olive oil

2 onions, coarsely chopped

2 carrots, coarsely chopped

2 celery ribs, coarsely chopped

6 to 8 cremini mushrooms, trimmed, cleaned, and coarsely chopped

3 cloves garlic, smashed

1½ cups tomato paste

¼ cup prepared horseradish

2 cups dry red wine

4 bay leaves

1 thyme bundle, tied with butcher's twine

1 bunch of fresh chives, minced

2 tablespoons freshly grated horseradish

1 Preheat the oven to 375°F.

2 Season the ribs generously with salt. Coat a large wide pan with olive oil and bring to high heat. Add the ribs to the pan and brown very well on all sides—this is an EXTREMELY important step in the development of big brown flavors. It may take up to 20 minutes—don't rush it!

3 While the ribs are browning, put the onions, carrots, celery, mushrooms, and garlic in a food processor and purée to a coarse paste; set aside.

4 When the ribs are very brown on all sides, remove them from the pan. Ditch the fat, add a bit of fresh olive oil, and add the puréed veggies to the pan. Season generously with salt and cook over medium-high heat until the veggies are very brown and a crud has formed on the bottom of the pan, 8 to 10 minutes. Scrape the crud and let it reform. Don't rush this step.

5 Add the tomato paste and prepared horse-radish and cook, stirring frequently, until it starts to brown, 1 to 2 minutes.

6 Add the wine, bring it to a boil (BTB), and stir frequently to scrape the crud from the bottom of the pan (this is the big-money flavor). Continue cooking until reduced by half, 3 to 4 minutes.

7 Return the ribs to the pan and add enough water to barely cover the meat. Toss in the bay leaves and thyme bundle, cover the pan with aluminum foil, and cook in the oven for 2½ hours. Check the ribs every 45 minutes to make sure they are still covered in liquid; if the liquid has reduced too much, add more water.

Turn the ribs after about 1 hour and continue cooking.

8 Remove the foil during the last 20 minutes of cooking to let things get nice and brown and to let the sauce reduce. When the meat is done it should be very tender but not falling apart. To serve, remove the bay leaves and thyme bundle and spoon the sauce over the ribs and sprinkle with the chives and freshly grated horseradish for an extra kick.

Here's the beef!

PORK
MILANESE
& ESCAROLE SALAD WITH PICKLED
RED ONIONS, HAZELNUTS & PECORINO

SERVES: 4 · TIME: ABOUT 1½ HOURS, MOSTLY UNATTENDED

To me, absolutely anything fried is delicious. In this recipe I take a traditional crispy, crunchy, salty, fried preparation for chicken and apply it to pork. I serve the pork with escarole—the unsung hero of the salad world (I'm on a mission to popularize escarole). Then I toss some chopped nuts and pickled onions into the mix. My mouth is so excited it just doesn't know which way to go; there's crispy pork, crunchy escarole, salty sweet nuts, and bright acidic onions. So many different things are going on in this dish that even though it's super-easy to make, it's also incredibly exciting to eat!

MISE EN PLACE

FOR THE ONIONS

¾ cup red wine vinegar

1 tablespoon kosher salt

1½ teaspoons sugar

2 or 3 shots of Tabasco or other hot sauce

1 red onion, sliced into very thin rings

FOR THE PORK

1 cup all-purpose flour

2 large eggs, beaten with 1 tablespoon water

1½ cups panko (Japanese bread crumbs)

½ cup freshly grated Parmigiano

4 thick-cut boneless pork chops, butterflied and lightly pounded

Kosher salt

Extra virgin olive oil

FOR THE SALAD

½ cup freshly grated Pecorino

½ cup hazelnuts, toasted (see page 17)

2 tablespoons fresh Italian parsley, chopped

1 head of escarole, cut into bite-size pieces

Pickled Red Onions (recipe below)

Extra virgin olive oil

FOR THE ONIONS

In a medium bowl, combine the vinegar with ½ cup cold water. Add the salt, sugar, and Tabasco and stir. Add the sliced onions and let sit for at least 1 hour.

FOR THE PORK

1 Set up your standard breading procedure (see page 51): one bowl with the flour, one with the egg-water mixture, and one with the panko and grated Parmigiano combined. Have a baking sheet handy to hold the pork after breading.

RECIPE CONTINUES

2   Season the pork with salt. Using one hand for dry ingredients and one hand for wet, take each piece of pork through the breading procedure: Dredge it lightly in the flour, shake off the excess, dip it in the egg wash, then pack on the panko. Lay the breaded pork on the baking sheet and refrigerate for at least 1 hour.

3   Preheat the oven to 200°F.

4   Pour ½ inch of olive oil into a large sauté pan and bring to medium-high heat. Set up your drying situation next to the stove by lining a baking sheet with a couple layers of paper towels. Test to see if the oil is hot enough by sprinkling a bit of flour or a few bread crumbs into it. It should sizzle; if it doesn't—WAIT. Once the oil is hot, add the pork, working in batches so you don't crowd the pan. Cook the first side of the pork until golden brown and crispy, 3 to 4 minutes; turn and brown the other side. When the pork is done, lay it on the paper towels to drain off the excess oil and sprinkle with salt. Then keep the pork in the oven while you cook the second batch.

FOR THE SALAD

1   Put the Pecorino, hazelnuts, and parsley in the food processor and pulse until coarsely chopped.

2   In a large bowl, combine the escarole, hazelnut mix, and some of the pickled red onions; dress this mixture with olive oil and some of the pickling liquid and toss to combine. To serve, place a pork chop on a serving plate and top with the lovely salad.

Mmmmm—Milanese my way!

it's good to bread ahead! if you have the time, let the pork sit for about an hour to really set the breading, if you're in a hurry—skip it.

POLPETTI BURGERS

In Italy they don't eat spaghetti and meatballs. Instead they have what they call *polpettini*, or little meatballs (page 47). And when they want something bigger, they make *polpettone*—meatloaf. I figured, if they make little ones and a big one, why not make a medium-size one and throw it on a bun? This size is just right, and if I could have a burger this good every time I wanted one, I'd be a happy, happy girl.

MISE EN PLACE

Extra virgin olive oil

2 onions, cut into ¼-inch dice

Kosher salt

2 cloves garlic, smashed and finely chopped

½ pound ground beef

½ pound ground veal

½ pound ground pork

2 tablespoons fresh rosemary, finely chopped

½ cup freshly grated Parmigiano

¼ cup bread crumbs

1 large egg

4 large hamburger buns

4 slices Fontina cheese

Mayonnaise

2 cups baby arugula

1 large tomato, sliced

Pickled Red Onions (page 161) or 1 red onion, thinly sliced

1 Coat a large sauté pan with olive oil, add the onions, and bring to medium heat. Season the onions with salt and cook until soft and aromatic, 8 to 10 minutes. Add the garlic and cook for another 2 to 3 minutes, stirring frequently. Remove from the heat and let the mixture cool.

2 In a large bowl, combine the cooled onion mixture with the beef, veal, pork, rosemary, Parmigiano, bread crumbs, egg, and 3 to 4 tablespoons of water. Mix well and season generously with salt.

3 Make a 1- to 2-inch tester patty. In a small sauté pan, heat a bit of oil and cook the patty. When it's cool enough, taste it to make sure it's delicious—if it's not, reseason. When the tester tastes fabulous, form the meat mixture into four equal patties.

4 Preheat a grill or coat a large sauté pan with olive oil and bring it to medium-high heat. Cook the burgers for 4 to 5 minutes per side. Toast the buns on the grill or in the toaster. While the second side of the burger cooks, place a slice of cheese on top and let it melt.

5 Schmear each side of the bun lightly with mayonnaise, place a burger on each bottom half, garnish with the arugula, tomato, and onions (pickled or otherwise), top with the other half of the bun, and serve.

Burger-licious!

ROCKIN' PORCHETTA

WITH FALL VEGGIES

SERVES: 10 · TIME: ABOUT 4½ HOURS, MOSTLY UNATTENDED

In Tuscany, every town has a market day. This is when trucks carrying all kinds of delightful edibles pull into the center of town, open up their sides, and become little grocery stores on wheels. Of course my favorite truck was always the porchetta truck—who doesn't love a truck that sells a delicious crispy pork product?

Traditionally, porchetta is a whole pig that's been boned and cooked for hours, until the skin gets totally brown and crunchy and the meat becomes wonderfully tender. It's most often seasoned with garlic, sage, and black pepper—and while pepper is not usually how I roll, it's appropriate in this dish to keep the classic flavors intact. What is totally unique in my version is to cook the pork on a bed of autumn vegetables—they soak up the lovely porky juices and help create the ultimate one-pot dinner for a crowd. Be sure to save some leftovers for a sandwich the next day!

MISE EN PLACE

1 bunch of fresh rosemary, finely chopped

1 bunch of fresh sage, finely chopped

10 cloves garlic, thinly sliced

1 tablespoon crushed red pepper

Extra virgin olive oil

1 picnic pork shoulder with the skin on, bone out (save the bone!)

Kosher salt

Freshly ground black pepper

5 or 6 onions, sliced

1 pound fingerling potatoes, halved lengthwise

2 pints Brussels sprouts, halved

1 celery root, peeled and cut into ½-inch dice

1 bottle of dry white wine

1 thyme bundle, tied with butcher's twine

10 bay leaves

2 quarts chicken stock (see page 85)

1 Preheat the oven to 450°F.

2 In a small bowl, combine the rosemary, sage, garlic, and red pepper and add enough olive oil to form a loose paste. Rub the mixture all over the inside of the pork (be sure to get it in every nook and cranny). Sprinkle the pork generously with salt and pepper, then roll it back up into a bundle and tie it tightly with butcher's twine.

3 In a large roasting pan, combine the onions, potatoes, Brussels sprouts, celery root, and wine; season with salt and add the thyme bundle and bay leaves. Lay the pork bone in the pan with the veggies and nestle the pork on top of the bone and in the vegetables. Roast for 30 to 40 minutes, or until the skin starts to brown and get crispy.

RECIPE CONTINUES

4 Brush the pork skin with the pan juices and add the chicken stock. Continue roasting for another 3½ hours, basting the skin every 30 or 40 minutes. If the skin becomes too dark, tent the pan with aluminum foil, but remember, we want a nice, dark, crispy pork skin!

5 Remove the pork from the oven, cut off the twine (you don't want to floss and eat at the same time), and remove the pork skin—it will probably come off in one large, lovely crispy piece like a helmet! Use kitchen shears to cut the skin into pieces and make sure everybody gets some on their plate. Slice the pork and serve it over the vegetables, drenched in lots of porky pan juices.

That's my idea of pigging out!

i suggest asking your butcher to bone the pork for you - but be sure to keep the bone!

BRAISED
CABBAGE
STUFFED WITH SAUSAGE & FENNEL

SERVES: 4 TO 6 · TIME: ABOUT 2 HOURS

My mom used to make stuffed peppers, but I don't like peppers. What I liked was the stuffing. So I've taken my mom's recipe, tweaked it, and stuffed it in cabbage instead. I've also added chicken livers. The livers add an earthy richness that makes this dish super-special. If you don't like chicken livers—or think you don't—this is one time where you should get beyond the ick factor, accept that they're worth adding, and move on . . . because this dish rocks.

MISE EN PLACE

FOR THE SAUCE

1 onion, cut into large chunks

2 celery ribs, cut into large chunks

½ fennel bulb, tough core removed, cut into large chunks

3 cloves garlic, smashed

Extra virgin olive oil

¼ pound pancetta, cut into ¼-inch dice

2 teaspoons fennel seeds, toasted and ground (see page 17)

Pinch of crushed red pepper

1 cup dry white wine

1 28-ounce can Italian plum tomatoes, passed through a food mill

2 cups chicken stock (see page 85)

2 bay leaves

Kosher salt

FOR THE CABBAGE AND STUFFING

¼ cup red wine vinegar

Kosher salt

1 large head savoy cabbage, leaves separated and tough bottom ribs removed

Extra virgin olive oil

1 onion, cut into ¼-inch dice

½ fennel bulb, tough core removed, cut into ¼-inch dice

Pinch of crushed red pepper

3 cloves garlic, smashed and finely chopped

1 pound fennel sausage, casings removed

½ to ¾ cup bread crumbs

½ cup freshly grated Parmigiano

3 chicken livers, finely chopped (optional but highly recommended!)

1 large egg

FOR THE SAUCE

1 In a food processor, purée the onion, celery, fennel, and garlic to a coarse paste.

2 Coat a large wide pan with olive oil and add the pancetta; bring to medium heat and cook until brown and crispy, 4 to 6 minutes.

3 Add the puréed veggies, ground fennel seeds, and red pepper and cook until the vegetables become soft and aromatic and start to brown, 8 to 10 minutes.

4 Add the wine, bring to a boil (BTB), and reduce by half, 3 to 4 minutes.

5 Add the tomatoes, chicken stock, and bay leaves and season with salt. Bring to a boil (BTB) and reduce to a simmer (RTS); cook for 15 minutes. Taste to make sure it's delicious; adjust the seasoning as needed.

RECIPE CONTINUES

1 Add the vinegar to large pot of well-salted water, bring it to a boil (BTB), and set up a large bowl of well-salted ice water. Add the cabbage to the boiling water and cook for 3 to 4 minutes or until just tender; immediately plunge it into the salty ice water. When the leaves are cool, remove them from the water and pat dry. Reserve.

2 Coat a large sauté pan with olive oil. Add the onion, fennel, and red pepper and season with salt. Bring the pan to medium heat and cook the vegetables until soft and aromatic, 8 to 10 minutes. Add the garlic and cook for another 2 to 3 minutes. Turn off the heat and let the mixture cool.

3 In a large bowl, combine the sausage, bread crumbs, Parm, chicken livers (if using), and egg. Season with salt, add ½ cup water, and mix well to combine; if the mixture seems too dry, add up to another ½ cup water—it should be kind of wet. Stir in the onion-fennel mixture.

4 Make a 1- to 2-inch tester patty. In a small sauté pan, heat a bit of oil and cook the patty. When it's cool enough, taste it to make sure it's delicious—if it's not, reseason.

5 Lay each cabbage leaf on a flat work surface. Spoon about ¼ cup of filling into each leaf. Fold the outside edges in and roll the leaf around the stuffing. Place each roll on the work surface with the seam side down so the roll will hold itself shut. Look at us, always thinking!

6 Add the cabbage rolls to the sauce, cover, and simmer for 15 minutes, then uncover and simmer for another 15 to 20 minutes, or until the sauce has reduced and thickened. Taste and adjust the seasoning. Serve the cabbage rolls with the sauce spooned over them.

Coolio—stuffed cabbage!

PORK CHOPS

SERVES: 6 · TIME: ABOUT 30 MINUTES ACTIVE TIME AFTER 2 DAYS IN THE BRINE

I grew up hating pork chops. My mom used to make pork chops that were about as fat as a piece of paper (that's all that was available back then), and she would cook them for a really long time—until they were dry and flavorless. Sadly, today so much commercially raised pork has so little fat in it that even if you cook it correctly, it can still be like eating your shoe. That's why I love this brine—it infuses the pork with moisture and flavor, so you end up with a succulent and delicious chop. Then I crust it with one of my super-secret flavor weapons—fennel pollen. I discovered fennel pollen when I was working in Tuscany; it's expensive but is so worth it. (If you can't find it or don't want to fork out the cash, toasted ground fennel seed is an acceptable substitute.) This is such a great combination of flavors that you will never think of pork chops the same way again!

MISE EN PLACE

3 to 4 tablespoons kosher salt

2 to 3 tablespoons sugar

2 tablespoons fennel seeds

2 tablespoons coriander seeds

1 teaspoon crushed red pepper

3 bay leaves

1 onion, cut into ½-inch dice

2 carrots, cut into ½-inch dice

2 celery ribs, cut into ½-inch dice

4 cloves garlic, smashed

6 bone-in pork loin chops (nice fatties!)

2 tablespoons wild fennel pollen (or substitute toasted ground fennel seeds)

ANNE ALERT!

This is a plan-ahead recipe! The brine takes a couple of days, but it's really worth the effort.

1 In a large bowl, combine 2 quarts water with the salt, sugar, fennel seeds, coriander seeds, red pepper, bay leaves, onion, carrots, celery, and garlic. (The amount of salt and sugar you use depends on your personal taste.) Submerge the pork chops in the brine, cover, and refrigerate for 2 days (if you don't have 2 days,

at least brine the chops overnight). Remove the chops from the brine, discard the brine, and cook these bad boys!

2 Preheat the grill to medium-high.

3 Roll the fat edge of each pork chop in the fennel pollen.

4 Place the chops on the grill over medium-high heat and cook for 3 to 4 minutes. Rotate the chops 90 degrees to create beautiful crosshatched grill marks; continue to cook for another 3 to 4 minutes. Turn the chops over

and repeat this process on the second side. If the chops start to burn, move them to a cooler part of the grill. Stand the chops up and grill the fat edge—you want to get it nice and crispy and release the lovely aroma of the fennel pollen.

Remove the chops from the grill and let them rest in a warm place for 8 to 10 minutes before serving. The meat should be pink in the middle and very juicy.

Juicy pork chops? Who knew!!!

RACK OF LAMB
CRUSTED WITH BLACK OLIVES

SERVES: 6 · TIME: ABOUT 30 MINUTES

I'm a big fan of nice, thick lamb chops—and I'm an even bigger fan of nice, thick lamb chops deliciously browned all over! That's exactly what you get with this recipe. Since you remove two bones from an eight-bone rack, these babies are thicker than a normal lamb chop. And, because you sear the chops on both sides—and the fat edge—before schmearing them with the lovely olive purée and finishing them in the oven, the inside stays tender and juicy, and the outside gets a beautiful, delicious, brown crust. Why is that so important? Because brown food tastes good!

MISE EN PLACE

1 cup kalamata or gaeta olives, pitted

½ bunch of fresh oregano, leaves finely chopped

1 clove garlic, smashed

Zest of 1 lemon

Pinch of crushed red pepper

Extra virgin olive oil

1 8-bone rack of lamb

Kosher salt

1 In a food processor, combine the olives, oregano, garlic, lemon zest, and red pepper. While the machine is running, drizzle in enough olive oil to create a smooth paste. Taste it—it should be olive-y and delicious!

2 Preheat the oven to 425°F.

3 Using a sharp knife and working from either end, remove the second and seventh bones from the lamb to make it a 6-rib rack; then cut 6 even chops, season them with salt, and let sit for 10 to 15 minutes.

4 Coat a large sauté pan with olive oil and bring to medium-high heat. Working in batches (if you crowd the pan the chops will steam instead of sear), add the chops and cook, turning once, until beautifully brown, 2 to 3 minutes per side. Then brown the fatty outside edge as well for another 2 minutes—SOOOOO delicious!

5 When all the chops are done, schmear them generously with the olive purée. Put the chops on a baking sheet and roast for 5 to 6 minutes for medium rare (7 to 8 for medium). Then let them rest for 4 or 5 minutes before digging in.

Lovely and lamby!

if you're making this for a dinner party, the browning
and schmearing can be done ahead of time and the
chops can be tossed in the oven just before serving.

BRAISED LAMB SHANKS

SERVES: 4 · TIME: ABOUT 3½ HOURS

I'm gonna jump right out there and say that lamb is my favorite meat. And this is probably my favorite dish—to both cook and eat. I love that lamb shanks look like something out of the *Flintstones*, even though one shank is the perfect size for one person. On a cold winter night when I'm home making dinner for my family, this is definitely my go-to recipe. Like any braise, it takes a bit of effort to get started, but once you get them going, you can just toss the shanks in the oven and let them go on their lamby way.

MISE EN PLACE

4 lamb shanks
Kosher salt
Extra virgin olive oil
2 onions, coarsely chopped

4 carrots, coarsely chopped
4 celery ribs, coarsely chopped
4 cloves garlic, smashed
1 cup tomato paste
2 cups red wine

2 tablespoons fresh rosemary, finely chopped
4 bay leaves
1 thyme bundle, tied with butcher's twine

1   Preheat the oven to 400°F.

2   Season the lamb generously with salt. Coat a large sauté pan with olive oil and bring to medium-high heat. Add the lamb to the pan and brown well on all sides; this may take up to 20 minutes. This is an incredibly important step—it's where all the big brown flavors start to develop—DON'T rush it.

3   While the lamb is browning, put the onions, carrots, celery, and garlic in a food processor and purée to a coarse paste; reserve.

4   When the lamb shanks are very brown on all sides, remove them from the pan and transfer to a roasting pan. Ditch the fat, add a bit of fresh olive oil to the sauté pan, and add the puréed veggies. Season generously with salt, and cook until the veggies are very brown and a crud has formed on the bottom of the pan, 8 to 10 minutes. Scrape the crud and let it reform. Don't rush this step.

5   Add the tomato paste and cook, stirring frequently, until it starts to brown, 1 to 2 minutes.

RECIPE CONTINUES

BROWNING AND BRAISING: Because Brown Food Tastes Good!

When I was in culinary school, I didn't get braising; it seemed like a pain in the neck. I had to go through so many steps to get started and I just didn't think it was worth the trouble. Now that I get it, it's my favorite cooking technique by far. Trust me: Braising is the technique that will showcase your skill as a cook! It doesn't matter what you're braising—if you follow my method you will make a beautiful, brown braise every time.

First, season generously and brown your protein well—whether it's a shank or a short rib, take your time. This is where the first big brown flavors develop and it takes patience—so don't rush it. What's important at this point is what's happening in your pan, not on the clock.

Once your meat is nice and brown, remove it, ditch the fat, add a splash of fresh olive oil to the pan, add your puréed veggies, and season again. These vegetables are what we call *soffritto* and they're the base of almost all braised dishes. Like the meat, you want to brown the crap out of the soffritto. Cook it until you see a crud start to form on the bottom of the pan, then scrape off the crud and let it form again. This is where we take things to the edge of disaster and yank them back. Food is the most flavorful one step before disaster!

After the soffritto is nice and brown, add your wine and tomato paste. Let the wine reduce by half, toss the protein back in the pan, and add enough water to cover it by about two-thirds—it should be nice and soupy. Then toss in a thyme bundle and bay leaves, bring it to a boil (BTB), reduce it to a simmer (RTS), and cook until things are nice and tender, usually a couple of hours.

Properly braised food should be very tender but still maintain its integrity and shape—it should NOT be falling off the bone. So check your braise along the way, and if the liquid level gets low, add a bit more water until the meat is perfectly tender and the sauce is super-flavorful. Follow this basic braising technique and your brown food will taste great . . . every time!

6 Add the wine, bring it to a boil (BTB), and stir frequently to scrape the crud from the bottom of the pan (this is the big-money flavor). Continue cooking until reduced by half, 3 to 4 minutes.

7 Add 3 to 4 cups water to the pan and stir to loosen the mixture. Taste to make sure it's delicious and reseason if needed. It will by no means be done, but it should taste good. Pour this over the shanks in the roasting pan. The liquid should come two-thirds of the way up the shanks; if it doesn't add more water. Toss in the rosemary, bay leaves, and thyme bundle, cover with aluminum foil, and cook in the oven for 2½ to 3 hours. Check the shanks every 45 minutes, turn them, and if the liquid has reduced significantly, add more water. When the meat is done, it will be very tender but not falling off the bone.

8 Remove the foil for the last 30 minutes of cooking time for maximum browning and to allow the liquid to reduce and thicken up. Serve with lots of sauce.

Lamb-bucco!

WHOLE
BRAISED VEAL
SHANKS

SERVES: 4 TO 6 · TIME: ABOUT 3½ HOURS

When I was working in Tuscany I made this dish every day. It's a traditional osso bucco, but instead of using cross-sections, it uses the whole shank. I love it this way—big and meaty—but if you want to make these into individual portions, have the butcher cut the shanks into cross-sections for you.

Because it's a basic braise, you get started the way you would with any braise—by browning the meat really well and then browning the veggies. The big difference here is I've added apples to the soffritto for a little something special. SWEET!

MISE EN PLACE

5 cloves garlic, 2 smashed and finely chopped, 3 just smashed

¼ cup finely chopped fresh rosemary

2 whole veal shanks

Kosher salt

Extra virgin olive oil

2 onions, coarsely chopped

2 carrots, coarsely chopped

3 celery ribs, coarsely chopped

2 Granny Smith apples, cored and coarsely chopped

1 cup tomato paste

2 cups dry white wine

2 bay leaves

1 thyme bundle, tied with butcher's twine

1   Preheat the oven to 400°F.

2   On a cutting board, use the side of your chef's knife to smash together the chopped garlic and the rosemary to make a coarse paste. Cut several deep holes in the veal shanks with a paring knife—really stab them! Using your index finger, stuff the holes with the rosemary-garlic mixture; this will perfume the shanks with a beautiful aroma while they braise.

3   Season the shanks generously with salt. Coat a large sauté pan with olive oil and bring to high heat. Add the shanks to the pan and brown well on all sides; this may take up to 20 minutes. Don't skimp on this step—this is where the big, rich, brown flavors start to develop, so take your time!

4   While the shanks are browning, put the onions, carrots, celery, apples, and the remaining 3 cloves of smashed garlic in a food processor and purée to a coarse paste; reserve.

RECIPE CONTINUES

5 When the shanks are very brown, transfer them to a roasting pan. Ditch the fat, add a bit of fresh olive oil, and add the puréed veggies and apples to the sauté pan. Season generously with salt and cook until the mixture is very brown and aromatic, 8 to 10 minutes. Again, don't skimp here—you want the veggies to form a crust on the bottom of the pan. This is where more of that lovely brown flavor develops, so take your time.

6 Add the tomato paste and cook, stirring frequently, until it starts to brown, 1 to 2 minutes.

7 Add the wine, bring it to a boil (BTB), and stir frequently until reduced by half, 3 to 4 minutes. Then transfer everything to the roasting pan with the shanks. Add about ½ cup water to the sauté pan to help release any of that good crud stuck to the bottom, then add it to the roasting pan.

8 Add 4 to 5 more cups water to the roasting pan and stir to combine; the mix should be pretty soupy. Taste and add more salt if needed, then toss in the bay leaves and the thyme bundle.

9 Put the pan in the oven and cook for 2½ to 3 hours, turning the shanks every 30 minutes, stirring and adding more water if the liquid reduces too much. If the shanks brown too much during the cooking time, tent the pan with aluminum foil. When the shanks are done they should be incredibly tender and flavorful.

Big meat!

SEARED
RED SNAPPER
WITH SICILIAN CAULIFLOWER
& PARSLEY SALAD

To me cauliflower is an underappreciated vegetable, and for no good reason. It's one of my very favorites and I return to it again and again for many different preparations. I love it because you can cook it to death, literally hammer it, and it just gets better! I find it goes absolutely beautifully with seared fish and a bright parsley salad—this dish is ballsy, bold, and rustic all at the same time.

MISE EN PLACE

FOR THE CAULIFLOWER

Extra virgin olive oil

2 onions, cut into ¼-inch dice

Kosher salt

Pinch of crushed red pepper

4 cloves garlic, sliced thin

1 28-ounce can Italian plum tomatoes, passed through a food mill

1 head of cauliflower, coarsely chopped

Grated zest and juice of 1 lemon (juice reserved for the salad)

¼ cup gaeta or kalamata olives, slivered

¼ cup caperberries, sliced into thin rounds

FOR THE FISH AND SALAD

4 6- to 8-ounce red snapper fillets with skin

Kosher salt

Extra virgin olive oil

Leaves from 1 bunch of fresh Italian parsley

Big fat finishing oil

FOR THE CAULIFLOWER

1 Coat a large saucepan with olive oil, add the onions, and bring to medium heat. Add a generous pinch of salt and the red pepper. Cook until the onions are soft and aromatic, 8 to 10 minutes. Add the garlic and cook for another 2 to 3 minutes. Add the tomatoes and ¾ cup water; season with salt. Bring the mixture to a boil (BTB), reduce to a simmer (RTS), and cook for 20 to 30 minutes. Taste it and make sure it's delicious.

2 Bring a large pot of water to a boil and season generously with salt; it should taste like the ocean. Add the cauliflower, let the water come back to a rolling boil, and cook for another 5 to 7 minutes, or until it's really soft and almost falling apart.

3 Strain the cauliflower and add it to the tomato mixture. Cook everything for 20 to 30 minutes more, or until the cauliflower has completely broken up and the sauce clings to it.

RECIPE CONTINUES

Taste and adjust the seasoning if needed. Stir in the lemon zest, olives, and caperberries; remove from the heat and reserve. (This can all totally be done ahead of time, and while it's really great when made to order, this dish actually gets better when made ahead.)

FOR THE FISH AND SALAD

1 Take the fish out of the fridge 10 to 15 minutes before you're ready to cook. Pat the skin dry with a paper towel and season on both sides with salt.

2 Coat a large sauté pan generously with olive oil and bring it to high heat, almost smoking. Coat the UNDERNEATH of another smaller sauté pan with olive oil. Place the fish fillets skin side down in the larger sauté pan and gently place the other sauté pan directly on top of the fish. The purpose of this is to gently press the skin of the fish onto the bottom of the larger pan to create a lovely, even, crispy skin. (The first thing fish skin wants to do is stick to the pan, and the first thing cooks want to do is move it. Resist the urge; it will unstick itself when it's ready. This is where patience comes in—if you try to move it before it's ready, the fish skin will win every time.)

3 After a couple minutes, remove the top sauté pan to allow the steam to escape and the skin to get really crispy. As the fish cooks it turns from translucent to opaque—the idea is to cook the fish two-thirds of the way on the skin side and then flip it over for the last third of the cooking time. The rule for fish is 7 to 8 minutes per inch of thickness, a little less if you like your fish on the rare side.

4 Reheat the cauliflower mixture if necessary. In a medium bowl, toss the parsley with the lemon juice, some salt, and a drizzle of finishing oil. Serve the fish nestled in a mound of the cauliflower and garnish with the parsley salad.

That's snappy cauliflower!

CRISPY-SKIN BLACK BASS

SERVES: 4 · TIME: ABOUT 15 MINUTES

Crispy fish skin is a treat. When done right, it's crunchy and salty, and tastes like the ocean. I've come up with this method for getting fish skin perfectly crispy because in my career I've spent a lot of time being frustrated by sticking fish skin to the pan. My solution is more than a recipe; it's a technique. And it will work for any fish with skin. This approach is all about having a hot pan, patience, and my secret . . . *a second sauté pan*. Use my method and you will always make fish with delightfully satisfying and crispy skin.

MISE EN PLACE

4 6-ounce wild black bass fillets

Kosher salt

Extra virgin olive oil

1 Take the fish out of the fridge 10 to 15 minutes before you're ready to cook. Pat the skin dry with a paper towel and season on both sides with salt.

2 Coat a large sauté pan generously with olive oil and bring it to high heat, almost smoking. Coat the UNDERNEATH of another smaller sauté pan with olive oil. Place the fish fillets skin side down in the larger pan and gently place the other sauté pan directly on top of the fish. The purpose of this is to gently press the skin of the fish onto the bottom of the larger pan to create a lovely, even, crispy skin. (The first thing fish skin wants to do is stick to the pan, and the first thing cooks want to do is move it. Resist the urge; it will unstick itself when it's ready. This is where patience comes in—if you try to move it before it's ready, the fish skin will win every time.)

3 After a couple minutes, remove the top sauté pan to allow the steam to escape and the skin to get really crispy. As the fish cooks it turns from translucent to opaque—the idea is to cook the fish two-thirds of the way through on the skin side and then flip it over for the last third of the cooking time. The rule for fish is 7 to 8 minutes per inch of thickness, a little less if you like your fish on the rare side.

Now that's a crispy fish tale!

HALIBUT IN PAPER

WITH YUMMY SUMMER VEG

SERVES: 4 · TIME: ABOUT 30 MINUTES

Fish in paper is a classic preparation that will totally make you feel like a rock star in the kitchen. It's super-easy and it's all about the presentation. All you have to do is toss some veggies and white fish in a parchment package along with some wine, and let them steam themselves. When your guests open their packages, they get a big burst of aromatic vapor and a lovely piece of gently cooked fish on perfectly cooked veggies. Just remember that because you seal the packages, you only get one shot to season everything—if you miss your opportunity then this will taste like a diet dish. You have to season well BEFORE you seal the deal.

MISE EN PLACE

2 zucchini, green part only, julienned

¼ pound haricots verts, sliced on the bias

2 plum tomatoes, seeded, guts removed, and julienned

½ red onion, thinly sliced

1 clove garlic, smashed and finely chopped

Pinch of crushed red pepper

Extra virgin olive oil

1 tablespoon fresh thyme leaves

Kosher salt

1 lemon, sliced

4 6-ounce halibut fillets

1 cup dry white wine

1 Preheat the oven to 500°F.

2 Fold four 9 x 13-inch pieces of parchment paper in half. Starting at the top of the fold, cut each piece into a large half heart shape (takes you back to Valentine's Day in school, doesn't it?). When the papers are opened, they should be the shape of full hearts. If they're not perfect, that's okay, but a big heart is always better.

3 In a large bowl, combine the zucchini, haricots verts, tomatoes, onion, garlic, and red pepper. Toss with olive oil and season with the thyme and salt. Oil and salt the halibut as well.

This is the only chance to season the veggies and the fish, so take advantage of it! Taste the veggies; they should taste good. If not, adjust the seasoning.

4 Open the parchment paper hearts and brush the paper with olive oil, leaving a 1-inch border.

5 Divide the seasoned veggies evenly between the parchment hearts, then lay the fish on top and place two lemon slices on top of each fillet. Close the paper in half over the fish. Working

RECIPE CONTINUES

from one end of the parchment to the other, fold the bottom of the paper over the top to create a closure. The seal needs to be really secure so the steam won't escape during the cooking process. Before the package is completely sealed, carefully pour an equal amount of wine into each and complete the enclosure. Put the packages on a baking sheet and cook for 8 to 9 minutes.

6 Remove the packages from the oven and place each one on a serving dish. Give each diner the chance to slice open their own package so they can enjoy the burst of aromatic steam that will be released—it's like a fish facial!

I heart you!

parchment is traditional here, but you can use aluminum foil to wrap your fish and it will work just fine - even easier to seal!

WHOLE ROASTED FISH
WITH SLICED POTATOES, OLIVES & HERBS

SERVES: 4 · TIME: ABOUT 1 HOUR

Making a whole fish is so cinchy that it's almost not fair. It looks like you've put so much time and effort into it, and it's so elegant and beautiful on a serving platter, but really, all you have to do is jam a fish full of herbs and lemon and toss it in the oven until its eyeball pops out! I think this is the coolest part—Mother Nature's own pop-up timer—I bet that's how they invented the pop-up turkey timer!

MISE EN PLACE

3 or 4 Yukon gold potatoes, sliced ⅛ inch thick (a mandoline works well here)

6 cloves garlic, 4 smashed and finely chopped, 2 just smashed

1 bunch of fresh oregano, half with leaves finely chopped, half as whole sprigs

½ cup gaeta or kalamata olives, slivered

Pinch of crushed red pepper

Extra virgin olive oil

Kosher salt

1 3-pound fish, such as snapper or bass, scaled, gutted, and gills removed

1 lemon, sliced

3 fresh bay leaves

½ bunch of fresh Italian parsley

1 cup dry white wine

1 Preheat the oven to 400°F.

2 In a large bowl, toss the potatoes, chopped garlic, chopped oregano, olives, and red pepper; drizzle generously with olive oil and season with salt. Arrange the potatoes and friends in the bottom of a baking dish large enough to accommodate the fish. Roast in the oven for 20 minutes. Remove and reserve.

3 Make 3 diagonal slices about ½ inch deep on each side of the fish. Season the outside and inside of the fish with olive oil and salt. Place the lemon slices, bay leaves, whole oregano sprigs, parsley, and remaining garlic inside the body cavity of the fish.

4 Pour the wine over the potatoes, lay the fish on top, and toss the whole thing in the oven for 35 to 40 minutes or until the eyeball pops out.

5 Remove the skin and bones and serve the fish over the potatoes.

This is a showstopper!

when you buy a whole fish, tell your fishmonger you want to have it scaled, gutted, and gills removed — you really don't want to do this at home.

CH NO. 5

SIDES

{ the sparkle factor }

I think of sides as the supporting cast to a great meal. They're the players that help bring out the best in the lead and make the whole show really interesting. Sure, you can do a lot with cooking techniques and seasonings to make a piece of fish or a steak special, but to me what makes a really great main course are the creative, super-seasonal side dishes that come with it. When I eat out, I often choose my main dish based on whatever exciting sides accompany it.

WHEN I'M THINKING OF WHAT SIDES TO MAKE WITH A MAIN, I don't get hung up on the idea that you have to serve a protein with a vegetable and a starch. Throwing this way of thinking out the window frees me up to be more creative. Why can't I serve two (or even three) veggies with a piece of chicken? What's wrong with a salad and a veg, or even two starches? Great sides don't need to get paired up with a big hunk of meat at all—often they're good enough to be the star of their own show. Some of the recipes in this chapter are so freaking good

you may just want to serve a couple of them together with some crusty bread for dinner tonight!

I'm a big believer that you can do whatever you want in your kitchen. Breaking the rules is fun and it pushes you to try new things. And once you have permission to break the rules, why not break them all over the place? Think of what foods you WANT to eat together and don't worry about what you think you're SUPPOSED to put on the plate. Remember, there's an exception to every rule and you are the chef of your own kitchen!

Perfect Green Veg . . . Every Time

Cannellini Beans with Pancetta & Rosemary

Swiss Chard with Pancetta & Baby Turnips

Super Creamy Cheeeeesy Polenta

Brussels Sprouts Slaw

Stewed Zucchini with Tomatoes, Oregano & Pine Nuts

Chanterelles, Fava Beans & Spring Onions

Braised Baby Artichokes

Frizzled Brussels Sprouts with Pancetta & Walnuts

Spice-Roasted Cauliflower & Jerusalem Artichokes

Yummy Lentils

Potato, Prosciutto & Fontina Cake

Pommes Chef Anne

Sweet Potato & Apple Hash

Loosey Goosey Garlic Mashers

Herb & Garlic Roasted Fingerlings

Crispy Crunchy Duck Fat Potatoes

PERFECT
GREEN VEG . . .
EVERY TIME

··········· TIME: ABOUT 20 MINUTES, DEPENDING ON THE VEGETABLE ···········

This is more of a technique than a recipe, and it's the perfect method for cooking any green vegetable. The technique, called blanching and shocking, is the same no matter what vegetable you're making; only the cooking time will vary. The idea here is that you PARcook the veg first in boiling water (Get it? *Partially* cooked), then you stop the cooking process immediately by tossing the whole shootin' match in salty ice water. Once your veg is parcooked, you can finish it however you like—sautéed in olive oil and garlic, for example, as I do here. This method works for broccoli, broccoli rabe, haricots verts, green beans, sugar snap peas, English peas, fava beans, asparagus . . . as I said, anything green!

MISE EN PLACE

Kosher salt

Green vegetable, cleaned and prepped as desired

Extra virgin olive oil

1 or 2 cloves garlic or to taste, smashed

Pinch of crushed red pepper

1 Bring a large pot of well-salted water to a boil.

2 Set up a large bowl of well-salted ice water.

3 Toss the veg into the boiling water and let the water return to a boil. As soon as it does, test the veg for doneness by tasting a piece. If it is cooked as you like it, carry on—if not, continue to cook it for another minute or two. (How crisp or tender you like your vegetables is a matter of taste—YOU BE THE JUDGE!)

4 When the veg is cooked to your liking, remove it from the boiling water and plunge it IMMEDIATELY into the ice water; swish it around so it cools completely. When the veggies are COLD, remove them from the ice water and let the water drain off or pat them dry—otherwise they'll splatter when they hit the hot oil. (Everything up to this point can be done ahead of time—like yesterday.)

5 Coat a large sauté pan with olive oil, toss in the garlic and red pepper, and bring the pan to medium-high heat. When the garlic is golden and very aromatic, 2 to 3 minutes, remove it from the pan and ditch it—it has fulfilled its garlic destiny!

6 Toss the veggies into the pan, stir to coat them in the oil, and cook until just warmed through. Season with salt and taste to make sure they're delicious.

Green veg = great veg!

CANNELLINI BEANS

WITH PANCETTA & ROSEMARY

SERVES: 4 TO 6 · TIME: ABOUT 1¾ HOURS (AFTER OVERNIGHT SOAKING), MOSTLY UNATTENDED

I don't know if my love of beans comes from living in Tuscany or if I was Tuscan in another life, but I adore beans. And when I want a stick-to-your-ribs side dish, I immediately think of Tuscan white beans. They're creamy and delicious, and they say, "Put me with pancetta!" And I say, "Sure, I'd be happy to." Then I toss in a bit of rosemary (but sage would be SOOOOO good here too!) and serve these with a yummy porky main—or just on their own for lunch.

MISE EN PLACE

FOR COOKING THE BEANS

1 pound cannellini beans, soaked overnight (see page 55)

1 onion, cut in half, skin removed, hairy end left on to keep it in one piece

1 large or two small carrots

2 celery ribs, broken in half

3 cloves garlic

1 thyme bundle, tied with butcher's twine

3 bay leaves

1 piece slab bacon skin, prosciutto skin, or a couple slices of bacon

Kosher salt

FOR FINISHING THE BEANS

Extra virgin olive oil

½ cup pancetta, cut into ¼-inch dice

3 cloves garlic, smashed and finely chopped

3 sprigs of fresh rosemary, leaves finely chopped

Pinch of crushed red pepper

ANNE ALERT!

Due to the soaking time, this is definitely a plan-ahead recipe.

TO COOK THE BEANS

1 Drain the beans, put them in a large pot, and cover them with water by at least 2 inches. Add the onion, carrots, celery, garlic, thyme bundle, bay leaves, and bacon skin.

2 Bring the pot to a boil (BTB) and reduce to a simmer (RTS); cook for about 1 hour or until ALL the beans are soft, adding more water if it reduces too quickly. To test the beans for doneness, do the 5-Bean Test: Bite into five beans; if they are all soft, then the pot is done. (Beans do not all cook at the same rate, so tasting at least five is important.)

3 Remove the pot from the heat, season the water generously with salt, and let sit for 15 minutes. If you're using them right away, strain the beans, reserving at least 1 cup of their cooking liquid. If not using them immediately, refrigerate them in their liquid.

So . . . if you forgot to soak your beans last night, use the "quick soak" method: Put your beans in a pot and cover them with at least 2 inches of water. Bring the pot to a boil (BTB), turn off the heat, and let the pot sit until the water has cooled. Proceed with the recipe as if you had soaked the beans overnight!

TO FINISH THE BEANS

1 Coat a large, straight-sided sauté pan with olive oil and toss in the pancetta. Cook until brown and crispy, 7 to 8 minutes.

2 Add the garlic, rosemary, and red pepper and cook for 2 to 3 more minutes, or until very aromatic.

3 Add the beans and the reserved bean water (if you didn't remember to save the bean water, use 1 cup chicken stock or water). Cook until the liquid has almost completely evaporated. Taste and season with salt if needed.

Bean-a-licious!

SWISS CHARD

WITH PANCETTA & BABY TURNIPS

SERVES: 4 · TIME: ABOUT 45 MINUTES

As a kid I remember my grandmother talking about how much she loved Swiss chard, but the weird thing is, I never saw her eat it—ever. But she always had it in the garden and she attributed her good health, even in her old age, to eating Swiss chard. Coincidentally, her name was Gramma Green!

I find Swiss chard to be one of the most interesting and delicious greens around. Here I use both the stems and the leaves and mix them with turnips. People give turnips a bad rap, but I think it's just because they haven't experienced them. I realize I'm combining two ingredients in this dish that people might not think of eating on their own, let alone together, but I'm on a mission to make Swiss chard and turnips popular. And if any dish with chard and turnips can turn you on, I'm betting this one can!

MISE EN PLACE

Kosher salt

1 bunch of baby turnips, tops removed

Extra virgin olive oil

½ cup pancetta, cut into ¼-inch dice

2 cloves garlic, smashed

Pinch of crushed red pepper

1 bunch of Swiss chard, stems removed and cut into ½-inch lengths, leaves cut into 1-inch ribbons

½ cup chicken or veggie stock (see page 85)

1 Bring a medium pot of super-salty water to a boil. How do you know if it's super-salty? TASTE IT! Toss in the baby turnips, let the water come back to a boil, and cook until fork-tender, 8 to 10 minutes. Drain the turnips and let cool.

2 When the turnips are cool enough to handle, use a clean kitchen towel to rub the skin off. Cut into quarters and reserve.

3 Coat a large sauté pan lightly with olive oil, add the pancetta, garlic, and red pepper, and bring to medium-high heat. When the garlic has turned a lovely golden brown, 2 to 3 minutes, remove it from the pan and ditch it—it has fulfilled its garlic destiny!

4 When the pancetta becomes brown and crispy, add the turnips, chard stems, and stock and cook until the stock has mostly evaporated, 4 to 5 minutes.

5 Add the chard leaves and sauté until just wilted. Taste and adjust the seasoning as needed.

Gramma Green would love THIS Swiss chard!

SUPER CREAMY
CHEEEESY
POLENTA

SERVES: 4 · TIME: ABOUT 1 HOUR

For years polenta reminded me of the Cream of Wheat my mother used to send me off to school with in the morning. It was totally boring. But once I started making polenta for myself I discovered I LOVED it. My special twist? I fat it up with milk, Parm, Fontina cheese, and mascarpone until it's creamy, decadent, and delicious. Just remember, the kicker here is to season the liquid with plenty of salt in the beginning—it makes all the difference.

MISE EN PLACE

2 cups whole milk

1 bay leaf

Pinch of cayenne pepper

Kosher salt

1 cup polenta

½ cup freshly grated Parmigiano

½ cup freshly grated Fontina cheese

¼ cup mascarpone

½ bunch of fresh sage, finely chopped

1 In a medium saucepan combine the milk, 2 cups water, the bay leaf, and the cayenne. Season generously with salt—you want to take the seasoning to the edge of too salty in this case. To do this you MUST taste as you go! Polenta acts like a "salt eraser," and if you don't salt abundantly in this early step, you'll never be able to get it properly seasoned. Bring the pot to a boil (BTB).

2 When the liquid is boiling, gradually sprinkle in the polenta, whisking constantly. Once the polenta is combined, IMMEDIATELY switch to a wooden spoon and stir frequently until the polenta thickens; this will take 30 to 35 minutes. Taste the polenta to see if it's cooked through;

if it still feels mealy and grainy, add more milk or water and continue to cook for another 10 minutes. Repeat this process as needed until the polenta feels smooth and creamy on your tongue.

3 Remove the bay leaf and stir in the Parmigiano, Fontina, mascarpone, and sage. Serve immediately, or put a layer of plastic wrap right on the surface of the polenta (this prevents a skin from forming on the top) and reserve.

More polenta please!

BRUSSELS SPROUTS
SLAW

SERVES: 4 TO 6 · TIME: ABOUT 1¼ HOURS, MOSTLY UNATTENDED

Brussels sprouts are one of those things my mom made once when I was a kid. My sister—the perfect middle child—ate hers right up while my little brother and I sat there frowning at them. I think I was almost thirty years old before I gave Brussels sprouts a second shot. Now they're one of my favorite vegetables, and this dish is my special take on coleslaw.

MISE EN PLACE

2 pints Brussels sprouts, shaved on a mandoline or cut as thinly as possible

½ red onion, thinly sliced

2 carrots, grated on the large side of a box grater

1 Granny Smith apple, julienned

½ cup apple cider vinegar

2 tablespoons Dijon mustard

2 tablespoons honey

Kosher salt

½ cup mayonnaise

1 In a large bowl, toss together the Brussels sprouts, onion, carrots, and apple.

2 Combine the vinegar, mustard, and honey in a small bowl and whisk well.

3 Add the vinegar mixture to the veggies, season with salt, toss to combine, and let sit for at least 1 hour.

4 Stir in the mayonnaise, taste, and adjust the seasoning if needed (it probably will).

Now that's something to sprout about!

1/15/12

STEWED ZUCCHINI

WITH TOMATOES, OREGANO & PINE NUTS

SERVES: 4 TO 6 · TIME: ABOUT 1 HOUR

This dish reminds me of summertime as a kid. Growing up we had a vegetable garden and we always grew zucchini—one of those veggies that if you grow some, you get a ton. So my mom was constantly coming up with different ways to use all the zucchini we had hanging around—we had stuffed zucchini, grilled zucchini, zucchini bread, you name it. (I took more zucchini bread to my teachers at school than you can imagine!) This preparation of stewed zucchini was one my favorites. Zucchini with tomatoes and cheese . . . HELLO? What's not to love???

MISE EN PLACE

Extra virgin olive oil

1 onion, cut into ¼-inch dice

Kosher salt

Pinch of crushed red pepper

2 cloves garlic, smashed and finely chopped

1 14-ounce can San Marzano tomatoes, passed through a food mill or puréed

2 zucchini, cut in half lengthwise and then into ¼-inch slices on the bias

½ bunch of fresh oregano, leaves finely chopped

¼ cup pine nuts, toasted (see page 17)

½ cup freshly grated Parmigiano

1 Coat a large, straight-sided sauté pan with olive oil, toss in the onion, and bring to medium-high heat. Season with salt and the red pepper and cook until the onion is soft and aromatic, 8 to 10 minutes.

2 Add the garlic and cook for another 2 to 3 minutes, stirring frequently.

3 Add the tomatoes and 1 cup water, taste, and season with salt. Bring to a boil (BTB), then reduce to a simmer (RTS) and cook for 15 minutes or until the mixture has reduced by about half.

4 Stir in the zucchini, cover, and cook for another 15 minutes or until it is soft and pliable.

5 Remove the lid and toss in the oregano and pine nuts. Cook for another 5 to 10 minutes or until the excess liquid has evaporated and the zucchini is hanging out in a thick tomato sauce.

6 Stir in the Parm, taste, and adjust the seasoning if needed. Serve hot or at room temp.

Super squashy!

ANNE ALTERNATE String beans, Romano beans, or broccoli can be substituted for the zucchini.

CHANTERELLES,
FAVA BEANS
& SPRING ONIONS

Fava beans require some preparation, but to me it's a labor of love. Shelling and peeling them may seem like a drag, but it's SOOOOO worth the effort. Mix them with some luxurious mushrooms and sexy spring onions, and you end up with springtime on a plate. I love this combo so much I wish these veggies were in season all year long!

MISE EN PLACE

Kosher salt

1 pound fava beans, shelled

Extra virgin olive oil

2 spring onions, thinly sliced

Pinch of crushed red pepper

½ pound chanterelles, brushed clean and torn into bite-size pieces

¼ cup chicken or veggie stock (see page 85)

½ bunch of fresh chives, finely chopped

1 Bring a large pot of well-salted water to a boil and set up a bowl of well-salted ice water.

2 Add the fava beans to the boiling water and let the water come back to a boil, then cook the beans for another 2 minutes. Strain the beans from the boiling water and plunge them IMMEDIATELY into the ice water.

3 When the favas are cold, peel off the tough outer layer and reserve the lovely bright green beans. YUM!

4 Coat a large sauté pan with olive oil, toss in the spring onions, and bring the pan to medium heat. Season the onions with salt and the red pepper and cook for 2 to 3 minutes.

5 Add in the mushrooms, add stock, cover, and cook for another 2 to 3 minutes.

6 Remove the lid, toss in the reserved fava beans, and cook for 2 to 3 more minutes or until the stock has evaporated. Taste and adjust the seasoning if needed. Sprinkle in the chives and serve immediately.

Springtime-y delicious!

BRAISED BABY ARTICHOKES

SERVES: 4 TO 6 · TIME: ABOUT 30 MINUTES

Baby arties are much easier to prepare than big ones and you don't end up with nearly as much waste. They're a perfect side when they're in season—they go beautifully with meat or fish and just scream springtime. Whenever I tell people I'm making artichokes they go, "Ohhh! Artichokes!!!" They just *sound* exciting.

MISE EN PLACE

3 lemons

24 baby artichokes

Extra virgin olive oil

6 cloves garlic, smashed and finely chopped

3 anchovy fillets (optional, but highly recommended!)

Pinch of crushed red pepper

1½ cups dry white wine

1 thyme bundle, tied with butcher's twine

Kosher salt

¼ cup freshly grated Parmigiano

¼ cup bread crumbs

1 bunch of fresh Italian parsley, leaves finely chopped

1 Fill a large bowl with water. Cut 1 lemon in half, squeeze the juice into the water, and drop both halves into the bowl.

2 Trim the tough, dark green skin from the artichoke stems and remove the tough outer leaves until the lovely, tender inner green leaves are revealed; it should be only a couple of layers. Cut the arties in half lengthwise and toss them into the acidulated water.

3 Zest and juice the remaining 2 lemons and reserve.

4 Coat a large, straight-sided sauté pan generously with olive oil, add the garlic, anchovies (if using), and red pepper, and bring to medium heat. When the garlic is very aromatic and the anchovies have dissolved, 2 to 3 minutes, remove the artichokes from the water and add them to the pan along with the lemon zest, juice, white wine, and thyme bundle. Season with salt and add just enough water to cover the artichokes; bring everything to a boil (BTB), then reduce to a simmer (RTS). Cover the pan and cook for 10 to 15 minutes or until the artichokes are very soft. Remove the lid and let the liquid reduce until it comes less than halfway up the sides of the arties.

5 Remove the thyme bundle and toss in the Parm and bread crumbs. Swirl and stir to combine. Taste for seasoning and adjust if you need to (you probably will), and sprinkle in the parsley.

That's no 'choke!

artichokes will turn brown
(oxidize) before your eyes,
so before you peel off
even one leaf, be sure to
set up your bowl of lemon
(acidulated) water.

FRIZZLED
BRUSSELS SPROUTS
WITH PANCETTA & WALNUTS

SERVES: 4 · TIME: ABOUT 30 MINUTES

Historically, I have not been a huge fan of Brussels sprouts, but now I LOOOOOVE them—and I especially love them cooked this way. I'll admit this approach takes some time—you start by peeling all the leaves off the sprouts—but it's so worth it for the fluttery, frizzled fabulousness that happens once you cook them. Also, I find separating the leaves helps get rid of that cabbagey flavor that people who think they don't like Brussels sprouts complain about. Listen: If you think you don't like Brussels sprouts, try these; I've made a lot of converts this way. The salty deliciousness of pancetta, the crunchy nuttiness of walnuts, and the delicate little leaves make this something special—not like any Brussels sprouts you've ever had.

MISE EN PLACE

Extra virgin olive oil

1 clove garlic, smashed

Pinch of crushed red pepper

¼ pound pancetta, cut into ¼-inch dice

½ cup walnuts, coarsely chopped

1 pint Brussels sprouts, stemmed and leaves pulled apart

Kosher salt

1 Coat a large sauté pan with olive oil; add the garlic and red pepper and bring to medium heat. When the garlic has turned a lovely golden brown, 2 to 3 minutes, remove it from the pan and ditch it—it has fulfilled its garlic destiny!

2 Add the pancetta and walnuts and cook until the pancetta is crispy and brown, 5 to 6 minutes. Add the Brussels sprouts and toss to combine. Season with salt, cover, and cook for 2 to 3 minutes, or until the sprouts have wilted.

3 Remove the lid, raise the heat to medium-high, and let the sprout leaves brown and "frizzle," 8 to 10 minutes more. Taste and season with salt if needed.

Not your mamma's Brussels sprouts!

don't be hesitant about letting the sprouts brown— the darker & crispier the sprouts get, the better they taste!

SPICE-ROASTED CAULIFLOWER
& JERUSALEM ARTICHOKES

SERVES: 4 TO 6 · TIME: ABOUT 1 HOUR

Any recipe that includes cauliflower makes me a happy girl. In this dish I roast cauliflower (which is one of the easiest ways to cook it) together with Jerusalem arties (a.k.a. sunchokes), and the payoff is huge: You get great flavor and a really sexy texture. Then I add some spices. The end result is a super-special, slightly exotic side dish—with a minimum amount of effort. This is the way I like to roll!

MISE EN PLACE

1 head of cauliflower, cut into bite-size florets

1 pound Jerusalem artichokes, cut into 1-inch dice

Extra virgin olive oil

Kosher salt

1 tablespoon cumin seeds, toasted and ground (see page 17)

½ teaspoon cayenne pepper

1 bunch of fresh chives, finely chopped

---

1 Preheat the oven to 375°F.

2 In a large bowl, combine the cauliflower and Jerusalem artichokes; toss them generously with olive oil and salt.

3 In a small bowl, combine the cumin and cayenne and add it to the veggies. Toss well to thoroughly combine.

4 Spread the veggies on a baking sheet in one even layer—use two baking sheets if necessary. Roast for 20 minutes, then stir the veggies so they have the chance to brown all over, and rotate the pan to ensure even cooking. After 20 minutes, repeat this process again.

5 Roast the vegetables for an additional 5 to 10 minutes, or until they are brown, tender, and smell wonderful—almost like popcorn! If they aren't lovely and brown, let them continue to roast for another few minutes. Taste and adjust the seasoning if necessary.

6 Remove the veggies from the oven, sprinkle with chives, transfer to a serving dish, and serve immediately.

I'd eat a bouquet of this flower!

YUMMY
LENTILS

SERVES: 4 TO 6 · TIME: ABOUT 1¼ HOURS

Some people think of lentils only in terms of soup, but you can do a lot with the lowly lentil. Here I go for a classic flavor combo and add some beautiful bacon into the mix . . . as I always say, everything tastes better with bacon!

MISE EN PLACE

FOR COOKING THE LENTILS

2 cups green or black lentils

½ red onion, peeled, hairy end left on

½ carrot

1 celery rib

2 cloves garlic

2 bay leaves

1 thyme bundle, tied with butcher's twine

Kosher salt

FOR FINISHING THE LENTILS

Extra virgin olive oil

4 slices of bacon, cut into lardons

½ red onion, finely diced

Kosher salt

1 clove garlic, smashed and finely chopped

1 carrot, finely diced

1 celery rib, finely diced

½ cup reserved lentil cooking liquid

1 bunch of fresh chives, finely chopped

TO COOK THE LENTILS

1 In a large saucepan, combine the lentils, onion, carrot, celery, garlic, bay leaves, and thyme bundle. Add water to cover everything by about 2 inches. Bring the water to a boil (BTB) and reduce to a simmer (RTS); cook for 20 to 30 minutes, or until the lentils are soft.

2 Remove the pot from the heat and season the water with salt. TASTE it to make sure it is well seasoned. Let the lentils sit in the salty water for 10 to 15 minutes.

3 Ladle out ½ cup of the lentil cooking water and reserve. Strain the lentils. Remove all the veggies and aromatics and discard.

TO FINISH THE LENTILS

1 Coat the bottom of a large sauté pan lightly with olive oil, add the bacon, and bring to medium heat.

2 When the bacon has rendered a lot of fat and become brown and crispy, 5 to 6 minutes, add the diced onion. Season with salt and cook until soft and aromatic, 8 to 10 minutes.

3 Add the garlic and cook for 2 to 3 minutes more, stirring frequently.

4 Add the carrot and celery and continue to cook until soft and aromatic, another 2 to 3 minutes.

5 Add the cooked lentils and the reserved lentil cooking water. Cook until most of the liquid has reduced. Taste for seasoning and add salt if needed. Toss in the chives and serve hot or at room temperature.

Lentils and bacon, lentils and bacon, lentils and bacon, oh my!

POTATO, PROSCIUTTO &
FONTINA CAKE

SERVES: 4 · TIME: ABOUT 2 HOURS

I'm a huge fan of potatoes! Which is why I love this dish. It's the perfect base for poached eggs at brunch, to sop up the juices of a big rib eye steak (page 156), to complement my fabulous brined pork chops (page 170), or just for lunch. When this was on the menu at my restaurant and I was craving something porky, cheesy, and delicious, I'd have one of the line cooks fry up one of these lovelies for me to eat while I worked. Yum!

MISE EN PLACE

2 pounds Yukon gold potatoes, peeled and cut into quarters

Kosher salt

¼ cup heavy cream

¾ cup freshly grated Fontina cheese

½ cup prosciutto, cut into ¼-inch dice

2 large eggs

Extra virgin olive oil

ANNE ALERT!

These lovely cakes need to chill for at least an hour before cooking so if you want to really streamline the operation, make the cakes ahead (even the day before) and stick them in the fridge until you're ready to eat.

1 Put the potatoes in a large saucepan and cover with water; season the water generously with salt.

2 Bring the water to a boil (BTB) and reduce to a simmer (RTS). Cook the potatoes for 25 to 30 minutes, or until fork-tender. Drain the potatoes well.

3 In a small saucepan, heat the cream.

4 While the potatoes are still hot, mash with a potato masher, leaving them a little bit lumpy; stir in the hot cream.

5 Mix in the Fontina, prosciutto, and eggs and stir well to combine. Taste and add salt if you need to—you probably will.

6 Form the potato mixture into cakes about 2½ inches wide and ¾ to 1 inch thick. Put them on a baking sheet and refrigerate for at least 1 hour.

7 Preheat the oven to 375°F.

8 Coat a large nonstick sauté pan with olive oil and bring to high heat. Working in batches, brown the cakes on both sides, about 2 minutes per side. Place the browned cakes on a baking sheet and transfer them to the oven for 10 to 12 minutes, or until heated through.

You say potato—I say potato *cake!*

POMMES CHEF ANNE

SERVES: 4 TO 6 · TIME: ABOUT 1½ HOURS

This is my interpretation of the French classic, pommes Anna. It's just as elegant as the traditional version, but I've added Parm for a cheesy little twist. What's beautiful about this dish is how the outside gets a delicious crispy crust while the inside has a wonderfully delicate texture, thanks to the layers of thinly sliced potatoes. I also love that you can make one cake and then just cut it into individual portions—super-cinchy!

MISE EN PLACE

3 russet potatoes

Extra virgin olive oil

¾ cup freshly grated Parmigiano

Kosher salt

1 Preheat the oven to 425°F.

2 Working one potato at a time, use a mandoline to cut the potatoes into slices about ⅛ inch thick, or as thinly as you can. (Contrary to what you might have heard, you don't want to put the potatoes in water because this will wash off the starch—which will prevent them from sticking together. Just work quickly so the potatoes don't turn brown.) Coat an ovenproof 8-inch nonstick sauté pan with olive oil. Starting in the center of the pan, lay the potato slices in concentric circles. (You're going to flip this out of the pan eventually, so your bottom becomes your top—make sure it looks pretty!) Brush the layer of potatoes with olive oil and add another layer. Brush each layer with olive oil and sprinkle every second or third layer liberally with grated Parmigiano and salt. After each layer of potatoes, use a spatula to press down on the potatoes so they stay compact.

3 Bring the pan to medium-high heat. When a lovely brown crust has formed, shoot the pan in the oven for 20 minutes.

4 Remove the pan from the oven, place a lid on the top, and tip the pan to drain off any excess oil. This is an EXTREMELY important step—when you take the cake out of the pan to serve it, you don't want hot oil to pour out and burn you—YIKES! After the excess oil has completely drained off, flip the pan over so the cake is turned out onto the underside of the lid. Carefully slide the cake off the lid and back into the pan so the beautiful brown side is on top.

5 Return the uncovered pan to the oven and bake for another 15 minutes or until the cake is fork-tender. Cut into wedges and serve.

Now that's a hot potato!

SWEET POTATO & APPLE HASH

SERVES: 4 TO 6 · TIME: ABOUT 45 MINUTES

I'm a fan of anything called hash. When I was a kid my parents would make fried eggs for breakfast and bust out a can of corned beef hash—it was a huge treat. Now I jump at anything that reminds me of hash. In this recipe I mix together sweet potatoes, apple, onion, and, of course, a bit of bacon for my own take on hash—a bit sweeter and certainly healthier than anything from a can!

MISE EN PLACE

Extra virgin olive oil

4 slices thick-cut bacon, cut into lardons (see page 20)

1 onion, cut in ½-inch dice

2 sprigs of fresh rosemary, leaves finely chopped

Pinch of crushed red pepper

Kosher salt

3 sweet potatoes, peeled and cut into ½-inch dice

¼ cup maple syrup

1½ cups chicken stock (see page 85)

1 bunch of scallions, white and green parts separated and thinly sliced

3 Granny Smith apples, peeled and cut into ½-inch dice

½ cup pepitas (green pumpkin seeds), toasted (see page 17)

1 Coat a large sauté pan with olive oil, add the bacon, and bring to medium heat.

2 When the bacon starts to get crispy and brown, 5 to 6 minutes, add the onion, rosemary, and red pepper. Season with salt and sauté the onions until soft and aromatic, 8 to 10 minutes.

3 Add the sweet potatoes, maple syrup, and chicken stock. Cover and cook for 15 to 20 minutes, or until the potatoes are soft but not mushy. Remove the lid and let the liquid reduce by about half.

4 Add the scallion whites and apples and cook for 5 to 6 minutes, or until the apples are soft.

5 Stir in the scallion greens and pepitas, taste, and adjust the seasoning if needed.

Let's hash it out!

LOOSEY-GOOSEY
GARLIC
MASHERS

SERVES: 4 · TIME: ABOUT 45 MINUTES

I love me a mashed potato. Add a few cloves of garlic into the mix and you have lovely garlic mashers! Or for something really special, I substitute celery root for some of the potatoes.

Celery root is my mother's favorite vegetable, but in our little town in upstate New York it's not always easy to find. One year for Christmas I got a huge bag of celery root and put it under the tree for her. She says it was the best Christmas present she ever got! If you haven't tried celery root before, you're missing out—it's a big, craggy, knobby thing, it smells like celery, is slightly sweet, and has a wonderfully starchy texture kind of like a potato.

MISE EN PLACE

2 pounds Yukon gold potatoes, quartered

4 cloves garlic

Kosher salt

1 cup heavy cream

8 tablespoons (1 stick) unsalted butter, cold, cut into 8 pieces

1 Place the potatoes and garlic in a large pot, cover them with 1 to 2 inches of water, and season generously with salt. TASTE IT! (If the water is underseasoned at this point, you will have bland mashers—and that's just sad.) Bring the pot to a boil (BTB) and reduce to a simmer (RTS). Cook the potatoes until fork-tender, 20 to 25 minutes.

2 Drain the potatoes and garlic and pass them through a food mill or ricer while they're still hot. DO NOT use a food processor or blender for this step or you'll end up with sticky, gluey mashed potatoes.

3 While you mash the potatoes, put the cream in a small saucepan and bring it to a boil (BTB). Once the cream reaches a boil, remove from the heat.

4 While the potatoes are still hot add a third of the cream and a third of the butter and stir vigorously. Repeat this process twice more until all of the cream and butter is incorporated. Taste for seasoning and add salt if needed. Serve immediately or cover with foil and keep warm in an oven at low heat.

Mmmmm-ashers!

ANNE ALTERNATE Substitute 1 pound of peeled, chopped celery root for half of the potatoes and skip the garlic. Start with the celery root and boil it for 6 to 7 minutes in well-salted water, then toss in the potatoes. Proceed with the recipe.

HERB & GARLIC ROASTED
FINGERLINGS

Roasted potatoes can be snore city. But when you do them well, they're simple, totally rustic, and super-delicious. Fingerlings are perfect for roasting because they're small and creamy, but a mix of red bliss and white new potatoes cut into bite-size pieces works well too. Don't be afraid to use lots of olive oil, salt, and herbs here—and roast these lovelies until they're brown, brown, brown. Remember, brown food tastes GOOD!

MISE EN PLACE

2 pounds small fingerling potatoes, cut in half lengthwise

4 cloves garlic, cut into quarters lengthwise

3 sprigs of fresh rosemary, leaves finely chopped

6 fresh sage leaves, finely chopped

Pinch of crushed red pepper

½ cup extra virgin olive oil

Kosher salt

1 Preheat the oven to 400°F.

2 In a large bowl, toss the potatoes with the garlic, rosemary, sage, red pepper, and olive oil; season well with salt. Place the potatoes on a baking sheet.

3 Roast the potatoes for 15 to 20 minutes, give them a stir, and continue cooking for another 15 to 20 minutes or until tender on the inside and brown and crispy on the outside. Taste and season again with salt if needed.

Give me the finger-ling!

CRISPY CRUNCHY
DUCK FAT POTATOES

SERVES: 4 TO 6 · TIME: ABOUT 1 HOUR

This is where you want to break out that lovely duck fat—the liquid gold saved from making Duck Breast with Dried Fruit and Vin Santo (page 152) or Cheater's Duck Confit and Bitter Greens (page 154). If you didn't remember to save the duck fat or don't have any, you can certainly buy it. And in a pinch you can use olive oil.

Duck fat is fabulous for frying because it has a relatively high smoking point (it can get really hot before it begins to break down), so it will make your potatoes golden brown and crispy on the outside, light and fluffy on the inside, and REALLY tasty. Save your duck fat; it's worth it.

MISE EN PLACE

2 pounds new potatoes, cut into quarters

1 clove garlic, smashed
Kosher salt
½ cup duck fat

1 onion, finely diced
½ thyme bundle, leaves chopped

1 Toss the potatoes with the garlic in a large saucepan and cover with about 2 inches of water; season generously with salt. Taste the water to make sure it is seasoned appropriately.

2 Bring to a boil (BTB) and reduce to a simmer (RTS). Cook the potatoes for 20 minutes, or until fork-tender. Drain the potatoes.

3 When cool enough to handle, put the potatoes on a clean work surface and squash them with the heel of your palm. Reserve.

4 Add the duck fat to a large, straight-sided pan and bring to medium heat. Add the onion and thyme and season with salt; cook for 8 to 10 minutes, or until the onion is soft and aromatic.

5 Raise the heat to medium-high, add the potatoes, and use a spatula to press them down onto the bottom of the pan—give them a good squish! Let the potatoes brown, 6 to 8 minutes.

6 Scrape the potatoes off the bottom of the pan and turn them. Repeat this process until the potatoes are brown and crispy everywhere, 15 to 20 more minutes. Taste and adjust the seasoning if needed.

That's a jacked-up home fry!

CH <u>NO.</u>

DESSERTS

{ my sweeties! }

A lot of savory chefs think that pastry and dessert are an
entirely different world. They'll say, "I don't *DO* dessert."
I think that's a cop-out. Knowing some basic desserts is
absolutely essential to being a well-rounded cook. In fact,
when I was in culinary school, I learned the most about being
a technique chef (someone who understands the importance
of *how* and *why* you do something rather than just how to
follow a recipe) from one of my pastry instructors.

A LOT OF THE SAME TECHNIQUES USED IN THE SAVORY KITCHEN ARE ALSO USED IN THE PASTRY KITCHEN, and while you certainly don't need to learn how to make a ten-layer wedding cake with rolled fondant or how to make pulled sugar, there are some pastry basics you should know— like how to whip egg whites to peaks, make a caramel, or pull together a simple crisp. While *mise en place* is always important, in the pastry kitchen it's essential—and measuring correctly is a big deal here, too. When it comes to pastry, once you get going it's hard to go back and fix things, so being totally prepped and having all your ingredients and tools on hand before you start is key to success.

I'm a big fan of dessert, but I can't say that I have a sweet tooth. After dinner I usually want only one bite of something sweet. But as a savory chef I *like* to make dessert, and I don't think a meal is complete without one. I've included some of my very favorite desserts in this chapter. They're all accessible to new and more advanced cooks, and they're also very much in tune with my character as a chef: thoughtful, creative, delicious, and, of course, a bit outside the box.

Mom's Anise Seed Cookies

Lemon Curd Tart with Almond Crust

Hazelnut Cake with Nutella Mousse

Goat Cheese Cheesecake with Spiced Nilla Wafer Crust

Apple & Olive Oil Cake with Sautéed Apples
& Mascarpone

Pear Tarte Tatin with Shortbread Crust

Macedonia (My Super-Special Fruit Cocktail)

Juicy, Jammy, Jelly Tart

Zeppole & Chocolate Dipper

Tarallucci with Salty Caramel

Chef Anne's Dried Cherry & Almond Biscotti

Blueberry Nectarine Crisp

Maple-Pumpkin Bread Pudding

Strawberry-Raspberry Shortcakes

MOM'S
ANISE SEED
COOKIES

MAKES: 32 TO 36 · TIME: ABOUT 2 HOURS

I remember these cookies with annoyance and affection. Growing up, every year for my birthday my mother would send me to school with her anise seed cookies. Other kids got to bring cupcakes. I was the kid with the anise seed cookies. It's not that I didn't like these cookies—I loved them then and I still do. But back then I just wanted cupcakes like everyone else! Today I'm pretty psyched whenever I get a chance to munch on these lovelies. I even made a version of this recipe during an Iron Chef battle and they helped us win!

MISE EN PLACE

¾ pound (3 sticks) unsalted butter, at room temperature

1½ cups powdered sugar, plus more as needed

1 large egg

1 teaspoon vanilla extract

Grated zest of 1 lemon

1 teaspoon baking powder

Pinch of kosher salt

2¼ cups all-purpose flour

2 tablespoons anise seeds, toasted (see page 17)

1 cup turbinado sugar

1 In a large mixing bowl, combine the butter and powdered sugar. Beat until light and fluffy.

2 Beat in the egg, vanilla, lemon zest, baking powder, and salt.

3 Gradually incorporate the flour and anise seeds. When the flour is well combined, turn the dough out onto a clean work surface dusted with powdered sugar. Knead the dough two or three times until it comes together, then form it into a disk, wrap it in plastic, and refrigerate for at least 1 hour.

4 When you're ready to bake, remove the dough from the fridge and let it warm for about 10 minutes.

5 Preheat the oven to 350°F.

6 Lightly dust a work surface with powdered sugar and roll out the dough; it should be about ¼ inch thick. Cut the dough into desired shapes and place the cookies on ungreased baking sheets. Sprinkle each cookie with some of the turbinado sugar. Bake for 10 to 11 minutes, or until the cookies are just golden. Let cool and serve or store in an airtight container.

Thanks, Mom!

LEMON CURD TART
WITH ALMOND CRUST

SERVES: 8 TO 10 · TIME: ABOUT 2½ HOURS

Lemon curd is very elegant. For some reason people think it's difficult to make, but it's not—it's simple, quick, and has a lemony freshness and creamy texture that just screams, "Eat me!" In this tart, I pair the bright lemon curd with a nutty, crunchy crust—they're perfect partners. What a combo!

MISE EN PLACE

FOR THE CRUST

½ cup sliced almonds, toasted (see page 17)

8 tablespoons (1 stick) unsalted butter, cold, cut into pea-size pieces

¼ cup sugar

¾ cup all-purpose flour, plus more as needed

½ cup almond flour

1 egg yolk

Pinch of kosher salt

FOR THE LEMON CURD

Grated zest of 3 lemons

¾ cup freshly squeezed lemon juice

1¼ cups sugar

5 large eggs

Pinch of salt

12 tablespoons (1½ sticks) unsalted butter, cut into pats

FOR THE CRUST

1 Put the almonds in a food processor and pulse until pulverized.

2 Add the butter, sugar, all-purpose flour, almond flour, egg yolk, and salt and pulse, pulse, pulse until the mixture is the consistency of grated Parmigiano cheese.

3 Add 1 tablespoon cold water to the mix and pulse two or three times—the dough should start to come together in a ball. If the mixture is still very dry and crumbly, add 1 more table-spoon cold water. Check the consistency of the dough by squeezing a handful—if the dough sticks together, it's done. If not, pulse the dough with 1 to 2 more tablespoons water.

RECIPE CONTINUES

4 When the dough has come together, dump it out onto a clean, lightly floured work surface. Using the heel of your hand, schmear the dough straight forward and then roll it back with your fingertips. Repeat this process one or two more times, dusting with flour if it sticks. Form the dough into a flat disk, wrap it in plastic, and refrigerate for at least 45 minutes. (All this could have totally been done ahead of time—like yesterday or even last week!)

5 Take the dough out of the fridge 20 to 30 minutes before you're ready to use it and let it come to room temperature.

6 Preheat the oven to 425°F.

7 On a lightly floured work surface, use a rolling pin to roll the dough ⅛ to ¼ inch thick. Lay the dough in a 10-inch tart pan, pressing it gently into the pan. Tear off a little piece of dough from the edge and roll it into a "dough ball." Dip the dough ball in flour and use it to push the dough into the sides of the tart pan. Trim the edge of the dough by rolling the pin over the top of the pan to create a clean edge; remove the excess dough.

8 Gently line the dough with a piece of aluminum foil, pressing it into the sides of the tart to keep them tall and straight. Fill the tart with 1 pound of dry beans or rice, put the pan on a baking sheet, and bake for 10 to 12 minutes. Remove the beans and foil and bake for another 2 to 3 minutes, until golden and crisp. Remove from the oven and let cool.

FOR THE LEMON CURD

1 Preheat the oven to 300°F.

2 In a small saucepan, combine the lemon zest, lemon juice, sugar, eggs, and salt and whisk until it reaches a homogeneous consistency.

3 Place the saucepan on the stove and bring to medium heat. Cook, whisking constantly, until the mixture thickens, 12 to 15 minutes. Remove the pan from the heat and whisk in the butter 2 pats at a time, continuing to mix until well combined.

4 Pour the lemon curd into the prepared tart shell and bake until the lemon curd has set, 15 to 20 minutes. Let cool completely before cutting.

Lemony fresh!

HAZELNUT CAKE

WITH NUTELLA MOUSSE

SERVES: 6 TO 8 · TIME: ABOUT 1½ HOURS

I LOOOOOVE Nutella. I can happily eat it straight out of the jar, so whipping it up into a mousse and serving it with a hazelnut cake just makes sense. It's nutty, chocolaty, and creamy all at once—what's not to love? As far as I'm concerned, anything with Nutella sells itself.

MISE EN PLACE

FOR THE CAKE

12 tablespoons (1½ sticks) unsalted butter, at room temperature, plus more for the pan

1½ cups all-purpose flour, plus more for the pan

1½ cups unhusked hazelnuts, toasted (see page 17)

1 cup sugar

½ cup hazelnut paste

1 teaspoon vanilla extract

3 large eggs

1 teaspoon baking powder

Pinch of kosher salt

½ cup unsweetened cocoa powder

FOR THE MOUSSE

1½ cups Nutella

½ cup mascarpone or cream cheese

1 cup heavy cream, chilled

FOR THE CAKE

1 Preheat the oven to 325°F.

2 Butter and flour a 9-inch round or square baking pan.

3 In a food processor, pulse the hazelnuts until coarsely chopped. Reserve.

4 In a large mixing bowl, combine the butter, sugar, hazelnut paste, and vanilla. Using an electric mixer, beat until the mixture is light and fluffy.

5 Beat in the eggs one at a time.

6 Add the baking powder, salt, and cocoa and beat to combine.

7 Gradually add the flour, stopping the beater when it is just combined.

8 Fold 1 cup of the chopped hazelnuts into the batter, reserving the rest for garnish.

9 Transfer the cake batter to the prepared pan and bake for 25 to 30 minutes, or until a toothpick comes out clean when inserted into the middle of the cake.

10 Let the cake cool for 10 minutes, remove from the pan, and let cool completely.

FOR THE MOUSSE

1 In a large mixing bowl, combine the Nutella and mascarpone.

2 In another large bowl, beat the heavy cream to soft peaks (see page 234)—you can use an electric beater here or just a whisk and good old-fashioned elbow grease.

3 Add a spoonful of the whipped cream to the Nutella mixture and stir until you don't see any streaks.

4 Using a rubber spatula, fold a third of the remaining whipped cream into the Nutella mixture. To do this, lift the mixture gently from underneath, bring the spatula up, turn it over, and *fold* the mixture over as you rotate the

bowl slowly. You want to do this gently; the point is to keep it fluffy and not squish the air out of the whipped cream. Repeat this process two more times with the remaining whipped cream. You're done when you should have a fluffy, homogeneous mixture.

TO ASSEMBLE THE CAKES

1 Cut the cake into 3-inch squares or rounds and cut each of these in half equatorially.

2 Schmear the Nutella mousse on both the bottom and the top half of each of the hazelnut cakes, then give each of the cakes a light sprinkey-dink of the chopped hazelnuts. Place the top half back on the bottom and serve immediately.

That's just hazel-NUTTY!

GOAT CHEESE CHEESECAKE
WITH SPICED NILLA WAFER CRUST

SERVES: 8 TO 12 · TIME: ABOUT 1½ HOURS, PLUS COOLING TIME

My favorite thing about cheesecake is the texture. I like a dry, dense New York–style cheesecake over a light, creamy one. By using goat cheese in addition to cream cheese, this recipe gives me a fabulous texture that's slightly crumbly, a bit tangy, and has just the perfect hint of sweetness. Add to that a spectacularly spiced crust, and an old classic is totally new and exciting again!

MISE EN PLACE

FOR THE CRUST

6 tablespoons unsalted butter, melted, plus more for the pan

2 cups Nilla wafer crumbs

¼ cup sugar

½ teaspoon cinnamon

½ teaspoon ground ginger

2 grates of fresh nutmeg

Pinch of kosher salt

FOR THE FILLING

2 8-ounce packages cream cheese, at room temperature

1 12-ounce log of goat cheese

12 ounces sour cream

4 large eggs

1½ cups sugar

2 teaspoons vanilla extract

FOR THE CRUST

1 Butter a 9-inch springform pan.

2 In a large mixing bowl, combine the Nilla wafer crumbs, sugar, cinnamon, ginger, nutmeg, salt, and butter. Stir together until well combined and homogeneous.

3 Use your fingers to press the crumb mixture onto the bottom of the pan and about halfway up the sides. Reserve.

FOR THE FILLING

1 Preheat the oven to 350°F.

2 In an electric mixer with a paddle attachment, beat the cream cheese and goat cheese together until light and fluffy. Add the sour cream and continue beating until combined. Add the eggs one at a time, beating in each until thoroughly mixed before adding the next one. Add the sugar and vanilla and beat until just combined.

TO ASSEMBLE THE CAKE

1 Pour the filling into the prepared crust. Place on a baking sheet and bake for 30 minutes; rotate the baking sheet and cook for another 25 to 30 minutes or until the filling is set. If the filling starts to color, tent the springform pan with aluminum foil.

2 Remove the cake from the oven and let cool completely before serving (it continues to set as it cools).

Say cheese . . . cake!

the cake will continue to set as it cools, but it's best served after it has been refrigerated overnight and has really firmed up.

APPLE & OLIVE OIL CAKE

WITH SAUTÉED APPLES & MASCARPONE

SERVES: 8 TO 10 · TIME: ABOUT 1½ HOURS, PLUS COOLING TIME

This is a super-yummy cake that you can whip together easily once you've got your *mise en place* under control. Start by preparing all your apples at once—then just break off what you need to sauté for the cake first, and put the ones for the topping in a bowl off to the side. After you've grated the lemon zest for the cake, squeeze the juice from the lemon and toss it with the reserved apples for the topping—this adds flavor and keeps them from turning brown while you make the cake.

If you really have it together, you can make the topping ahead of time and keep it in the fridge until you're ready to serve the cake. You don't even have to serve the topping warm, but I think it's really special this way. Got leftovers? This topping is great over ice cream, on pancakes, or, of course, on second helpings of cake!

MISE EN PLACE

FOR THE CAKE

2 tablespoons unsalted butter

2 Granny Smith or other baking apples, peeled, cored, and cut into 8 wedges each

5 large eggs, separated, plus 2 additional whites

¾ cup granulated sugar

½ teaspoon cinnamon

Grated zest and juice of 1 lemon (reserve the juice for the topping)

¾ cup extra virgin olive oil, plus more as needed

½ cup Vin Santo

1 cup all-purpose flour

Pinch of kosher salt

FOR THE TOPPING

6 tablespoons unsalted butter

½ cup packed light or dark brown sugar

1 teaspoon cinnamon

6 Granny Smith or other baking apples, peeled, cored, and cut into 6 wedges each

¾ cup golden raisins

½ cup Vin Santo

1 cup mascarpone, at room temperature

¼ cup granulated sugar

FOR THE CAKE

1 Preheat the oven to 350°F.

2 Melt the butter in a large sauté pan over medium heat, toss in the apples, and cook until they begin to soften, 7 to 9 minutes. Turn off the heat and let cool.

3 In a large bowl, combine the egg yolks, sugar, cinnamon, and lemon zest. Beat the mixture with a whisk until very thick, very pale, and doubled in size, then whisk in the olive oil and Vin Santo. Gently whisk in the flour. Reserve.

4 Put all 7 egg whites and a pinch of salt in the bowl of a stand mixer (you can use a hand beater here if you don't have a stand mixer) and using the whisk attachment beat the whites until they form stiff peaks (see page 234). Fold one-third of the whites into the cake batter until just combined—to do this, use a rubber spatula to lift the whites gently from underneath, bring the spatula up, turn it over, and *fold* the whites over as you rotate the bowl slowly. You want to do this gently and quickly; the point is to keep as much air in the whites as you can. Repeat this process two more times with the remaining whites. You're done when you have a fluffy, homogeneous mixture.

5 Brush the sides and bottom of a 9-inch springform pan with olive oil. Transfer the

RECIPE CONTINUES

CHEF ANNE'S EGG WHITE (AND WHIPPED CREAM) PEAK-O-METER

Separating and whisking egg whites isn't hard—but it does take some practice. First, when separating eggs, make sure that absolutely no yolk gets into the whites. If you're going for yolks, it's fine to have some whites mix in by accident, but if you get even the tiniest bit of yolk in your whites, they will never whip up.

To whisk egg whites, always add a pinch of salt—this helps them whip up faster and fluffier. Also, use the second-highest speed on your mixer, not the highest; this allows the whites to whip up more slowly and gives them more backbone (if you whisk whites too quickly, they whip up fast and fall fast!). To know whether the peaks are soft or stiff, use my peak-o-meter test (which works for whipped cream too): After whisking, take the bowl and whisk off the mixer, swirl the whisk around in the whites, then pull the whisk straight out and pause—then, after a second or two, tip the whisk on its side. If the peak sticking off the end of the whisk bends over or tilts down, that's a soft peak. If it sticks straight out—that's a stiff peak!

cake batter to the prepared pan and arrange the sautéed apples in an even layer on top of the cake.

6 Bake for 45 to 50 minutes or until a toothpick inserted in the center of the cake comes out clean. Remove the cake from the oven, let cool for 10 minutes, remove the sides of the springform, and let the cake cool completely.

FOR THE TOPPING
1 Melt the butter in a large sauté pan over medium heat. Add the brown sugar and cinnamon and swirl or stir to combine. Add the apples and toss to coat well. Add the raisins and Vin Santo and cook for 8 to 10 minutes, or until the apples are soft but still hold their shape. Turn off the heat and reserve.

2 Meanwhile, combine the mascarpone and granulated sugar in a small bowl. TASTE! Mmmmm . . .

3 Serve a slice of the cake with the warm apple topping and garnish with a spoonful of the sweetened mascarpone.

We rock!

leave the apples in the pan to cool while you assemble the cake batter; then use the same pan to make the topping - look at me, thinking ahead and saving YOU some dirty dishes!

PEAR TARTE TATIN
WITH SHORTBREAD CRUST

SERVES: 6 TO 8 · TIME: ABOUT 2½ HOURS

This is the most amazing upside-down cake you'll ever make. And if you don't already know how, you'll learn to make caramel—which used to scare me to death. I always worried about burning it. But making caramel does not have to be an intimidating process—you just have to pay attention. You also want to remember that this is a flipper situation; you need to make the bottom of your tart look pretty because it's going to end up as the top.

MISE EN PLACE

FOR THE CRUST

8 tablespoons (1 stick) unsalted butter, cold, cut into pea-size pieces

¾ cup all-purpose flour, plus more as needed

¼ cup sugar

Pinch of kosher salt

Zest of 1 lemon

1 large egg yolk

FOR THE FILLING

¾ cup sugar

Juice of ½ lemon

1 cinnamon stick

1 pint heavy cream

4 tablespoons (½ stick) unsalted butter, cut into pats

12 seckel pears, peeled, cored, and halved

FOR THE CRUST

1 In a food processor, combine the butter, flour, sugar, salt, and lemon zest. Pulse until it looks like finely grated Parmigiano cheese. Add the egg yolk and 1 to 2 tablespoons cold water, and pulse, pulse, pulse until the mixture comes together into a ball. If it seems a bit dry, add 1 more tablespoon water and pulse a few more times.

2 Dump the mixture out onto a clean, lightly floured work surface and knead it once or twice, until it comes together in a smooth ball. Using a rolling pin, roll the dough out to an even circle, 11 to 12 inches in diameter. Transfer the dough to a baking sheet lined with plastic wrap and refrigerate for at least 45 minutes.

FOR THE FILLING

1 Preheat the oven to 425°F.

2 Place the sugar, 3 tablespoons water, the lemon juice, and cinnamon stick in a 10-inch ovenproof, nonstick sauté pan. Bring to medium heat and stir to combine.

3 Raise the heat to high and bring the mixture to a boil (BTB), brushing down the sides of the pan occasionally with a pastry brush dipped in water. After 7 to 8 minutes the mixture will begin to turn light brown. Swish the pan around gently to promote even cooking and cook the

RECIPE CONTINUES

DON'T FEAR THE CARAMEL!

Making caramel can be a little scary but once you get the hang of it, it's fun. Start by putting sugar in a large saucepan and giving yourself a couple of insurance policies—some acid, like lemon juice, and some water. These two ingredients help the caramel cook without recrystallizing or burning super-quickly.

Then bring the pan to medium-high heat and let it rip. When you see the sugar start to turn a shade of amber, don't walk away—things can go south very quickly and if the sugar burns, there's no recovery. Once the sugar is one shade past amber and heading toward brown, pour in the heavy cream, reduce the heat to low, and stand back—the mixture will bubble up like crazy. This is why it's really important to use a large saucepan—you don't want it to overflow when you add the cream and the mixture bubbles up. This stuff is molten!!! It can cause a really severe burn if you're not careful.

Once the bubbles calm down, swirl in the butter a couple pats at a time. Be sure not to add more until each addition is melted. You've made caramel!

mixture for 1 to 2 more minutes, or until it turns a deeper amber color. Keep your eye on this and don't walk away; the sugar can burn quickly if you're not paying attention.

4 Remove the pan from the heat, add 1 tablespoon heavy cream, and whisk to combine. Discard the cinnamon stick.

5 Whisk in the butter 2 pats at a time. The mixture will bubble up, but that's okay, just be VERY CAREFUL not to let it splatter and burn you. When all of the butter has been incorporated, begin to arrange the pears in concentric circles as neatly and prettily as you can—remember, you're going to flip it out.

6 Return the pan to the stove and cook over medium heat for 20 minutes. Remove from the heat.

TO ASSEMBLE THE TART

1 Remove the pastry from the fridge, carefully drape it over the top of the pears, and tuck the pastry around the edges of the pan. Bake the tart for 20 to 25 minutes, or until the dough is golden brown and crispy.

2 Let the tart cool for 10 to 15 minutes, then place a serving platter upside down on top of the pastry and CAREFULLY flip the platter and pan over, letting the tart fall gently out of the pan.

3 Place the remaining heavy cream in a medium bowl and, using an electric mixer or a whisk and good old-fashioned elbow grease, whisk the heavy cream to soft peaks. Slice the tart and serve garnished with the whipped cream.

What a pear!

ANNE ALTERNATE You can totally use apples here instead of pears. I recommend Granny Smith or any other tart, firm apple. I also recommend using fruit that's not quite ripe because it's going to get really soft as it cooks.

MACEDONIA
(MY SUPER-SPECIAL FRUIT COCKTAIL)

SERVES: 6 TO 8 · TIME: ABOUT 1¼ HOURS

It's pronounced MACH-a-donia and you can use any kind of fruit you want here—whatever you have in the house, or what looks best at the farmers' market. The fruits that I suggest in this recipe are ones that I love, but have fun coming up with your own signature mix. The key to this recipe is to keep it REALLY cold so it's totally refreshing and palate cleansing.

MISE EN PLACE

2 cups sugar

Zest of 1 lemon, removed in large strips with a peeler

4 cups assorted summer fruit (any combo of the following: peaches, nectarines, plums, cantaloupe, honeydew, watermelon, strawberries, raspberries, blueberries, or any other firm-fleshed fruit you like), cut into bite-size pieces

8 fresh mint leaves, cut into a chiffonade just before serving (see page 58)

1 pint lemon sorbet

1 In a medium saucepan, combine the sugar with 2 cups water and the lemon zest. Bring to a boil (BTB), then turn off the heat and let cool. (You have made simple syrup!) When the syrup is cool, remove the lemon zest.

2 Transfer the syrup to a large mixing bowl, add the fruit, and mix to combine. Cover and refrigerate for at least 1 hour—the idea is to serve this COLD on a HOT summer day.

3 Ladle the fruit into individual serving bowls and sprinkle with the mint.

4 Nestle a scoop of lemon sorbet in each dish of fruit. Serve cold!

I'll have another one of THESE cocktails please!

JUICY, JAMMY,
JELLY TART

SERVES: 6 TO 8 · TIME: ABOUT 2 HOURS, PLUS COOLING TIME

Think of this sweetie as a giant Linzer tart cookie. Use any flavor of fruit preserves that you want, add a bit of fresh fruit if you like, and have fun making a little crisscross lattice top! It's super-cinchy—the only thing to remember is to use really high-quality preserves.

MISE EN PLACE

2½ cups all-purpose flour, plus more as needed

¾ cup sugar

2 teaspoons cinnamon

Zest of 1 lemon

½ pound (2 sticks) unsalted butter, cold, cut into pea-size pieces

3 large egg yolks

1 12-ounce jar high-quality cherry preserves

1 cup fresh or frozen sour cherries, cut in half

1 large egg, beaten with 2 tablespoons water

1 In a food processor, combine the flour, sugar, cinnamon, and lemon zest and pulse to combine. Add the butter and egg yolks. Pulse, pulse, pulse! Check the consistency of the dough by squeezing a handful. If the dough sticks together, it's done; if not, add 1 to 2 tablespoons cold water and pulse again until it just holds together.

2 Dump the dough out on a clean, lightly floured work surface. Using the heel of your hand, schmear the dough forward and then roll it back with your fingertips. Repeat this process 1 or 2 more times, dusting with flour if it sticks. Divide the dough into two pieces in a one-third/two-thirds split. Form the larger piece of dough into a disk and the smaller piece into a rectangle. Wrap them both in plastic and refrigerate for at least 1 hour.

3 Take the dough out of the fridge 20 to 30 minutes before you're ready to use it and let it come to room temperature.

4 Preheat the oven to 375°F.

5 On a lightly floured work surface, use a rolling pin to roll the larger piece of dough into a circle about ¼ inch thick. Lay the dough in a 9-inch tart pan, pressing the dough gently into the pan. Tear off a little piece of dough from the edge and roll it into a "dough ball." Dip the ball in flour and use it to push the dough into the sides of the pan. Trim the edge of the dough by rolling the pin over the top of the tart pan to create a clean edge; remove the excess dough.

6 Gently line the dough with a piece of aluminum foil, pressing it into the sides of the tart to keep them tall and straight. Fill the tart with 1 pound of dry beans or rice, put the pan on a baking sheet, and bake for about 15 minutes. Remove the beans and foil and bake for another 2 to 3 minutes, or until golden and crisp. Remove from the oven and let cool.

7 Spread the fruit preserves in an even layer on the bottom of the cooled tart shell and sprinkle the cherry halves in an even layer on top of the preserves.

8 On a lightly floured surface, roll the remaining third of the dough into a 10-inch rectangle. Using a fluted pastry roller or a pizza cutter, cut the dough into 1-inch-wide strips. Lay the dough strips diagonally across the fruit preserves to create a crisscross pattern. Brush the bottom ends of each strip with a little egg wash and

press the strips into the sides of the crust to secure them.

9 Brush the top of the pastry lattice with the egg wash.

10 Place the tart back on the baking sheet and bake for 10 to 12 minutes, or until the top is golden and crisp. Remove from the oven and let cool completely before serving.

Oh cherry baby!

ZEPPOLE & CHOCOLATE DIPPER

MAKES: 25 TO 30 · TIME: ABOUT 45 MINUTES

Every time I go to a street fair or the New York state fair, I breathe in the smell of fried dough as it wafts through the crowd and just go crazy for it. So I couldn't help but come up with my own version of the classic zeppole. But of course I added my own sexy twist: a delicious chocolate dipper! With this dessert, your kitchen will be as popular as the zeppole stand at the state fair.

MISE EN PLACE

FOR THE ZEPPOLE

1 cup sugar

8 tablespoons (1 stick) unsalted butter

Pinch of kosher salt

1 cup all-purpose flour

3 large eggs

Zest of 1 orange

3 cups peanut oil

2 teaspoons cinnamon

FOR THE CHOCOLATE SAUCE

6 ounces semisweet or dark chocolate, chopped

¼ cup heavy cream

3 tablespoons unsalted butter

3 tablespoons light corn syrup

FOR THE ZEPPOLE

1 In a small saucepan, combine ½ cup of the sugar, 1 cup water, the butter, and salt and bring to a boil (BTB).

2 Reduce the heat to medium and add the flour all at once, stirring vigorously with a wooden spoon. Cook until the mixture forms a ball, has a slightly sweaty sheen to it, and pulls away from the pan, 3 to 4 minutes.

3 Transfer the mixture to a large mixing bowl and let cool for 3 to 4 minutes (the mixture does not have to be cold, just cool enough so it doesn't cook the eggs when added). Using an electric mixer or lots of good old-fashioned elbow grease, beat in the eggs one at a time; be sure each is fully incorporated before adding the next egg. Add the orange zest and beat for another few seconds to combine.

4 Pour the peanut oil into a large saucepan over medium-high heat; the oil should come 1½ to 2 inches up the sides of the pan. To see if the oil is hot enough, drop a little ball of batter into it. If it sizzles and floats quickly, you're good to go. If the batter burns or the oil begins to smoke, it's too hot, so reduce the heat.

5 While the oil heats up, combine the remaining ½ cup sugar and the cinnamon in a medium mixing bowl.

6   When the oil is hot, drop tablespoons of batter into the pan without overcrowding. Cook the zeppole until they rise and get very brown and puffy, 6 to 7 minutes. Use a slotted spoon to scoop the zeppole out of the oil. Shake off the excess oil, then toss them immediately into the bowl of cinnamon-sugar and roll them around. Transfer to a serving dish. Work in batches to finish the rest of the batter. If the zeppole begin to color too quickly, reduce the heat; if they aren't sizzling when they hit the oil, raise the heat.

FOR THE CHOCOLATE SAUCE

1   Fill a small saucepan with 1 inch of water and bring to a boil (BTB), then reduce to a simmer (RTS). Put the chocolate in a large heatproof bowl that will sit comfortably on the saucepan without touching the water (a double boiler setup). Bring the pan to medium heat and melt the chocolate. Add the heavy cream, butter, and corn syrup and stir until the chocolate has melted and everything is combined (this is a pretty quick process), then remove from the heat.

2   Transfer the warm chocolate sauce to a serving dish and serve it with a platter of the sugar-coated zeppole.

Dough that's fried just has to be tried!

TARALLUCCI
WITH SALTY CARAMEL

SERVES: 4 TO 6 · TIME: ABOUT 1 HOUR

This is my take on the lovely Neapolitan crackers called *taralli*—which are kind of like an Italian version of a pretzel. In this recipe I combine a basic spritz cookie with a caramel dipper and a sprinkey-dink of rock salt. These are more than just cookies—they are seriously addictive, super-cinchy, and guaranteed to make YOU a superstar when it comes time for dessert. Betcha can't eat just one!

MISE EN PLACE

FOR THE COOKIES

½ pound (2 sticks) unsalted butter, at room temperature

1 cup powdered sugar

1 teaspoon vanilla extract

1¾ cups all-purpose flour

Pinch of salt

FOR THE CARAMEL DIPPER

1½ cups granulated sugar

Juice of 1 lemon

¼ cup heavy cream

12 tablespoons (1½ sticks) unsalted butter, cut into pats

2 tablespoons rock salt (for eating—not for melting the ice on the driveway!)

FOR THE COOKIES

1 Preheat the oven to 325°F.

2 Place the butter, powdered sugar, and vanilla in the bowl of an electric mixer equipped with a paddle attachment (the one that looks like a peace sign). Beat the butter, sugar, and vanilla together until creamy and homogeneous, 3 to 4 minutes.

3 Remove the bowl from the mixer and, using a rubber spatula, fold in the flour and salt. Try to do this briskly without mixing the batter too much—mix until the flour is just combined.

4 Working in batches, transfer the batter to a pastry bag fitted with a large star tip. Pipe the dough onto an ungreased baking sheet in 2-inch circles.

5 Bake the cookies for 12 to 15 minutes or until golden. Let them cool completely.

FOR THE CARAMEL DIPPER

1 In a large saucepan, combine the sugar, lemon juice, and ¼ cup water. Bring the pot to a boil (BTB). Be careful not to swish the pan around too much at this point because it can cause the sugar to recrystallize. As the sugar mixture boils, the water will evaporate and the sugar will begin to turn brown, or caramelize. Be patient, this will take some time, 12 to 15 minutes. DO NOT take your eyes off the sugar! The sauce can go from golden to ruined very quickly. Relax and enjoy it—you're living on the edge and that's exciting!

2 Gradually the sugar will begin to turn gold, then light brown, and then one shade past light brown—this is when you want to remove the pan from the heat and immediately add the heavy cream; as you do this, the mixture will bubble up like crazy.

3 Whisk the cream until things settle down, then add the butter, two pats at a time. Be sure the butter is completely incorporated before adding more.

4 Once all the butter has been added, let the caramel cool. To serve, put 4 or 5 cookies on each plate with a little dipping dish of about ¼ cup of the sauce. Sprinkle the sauce with a few grains of rock salt.

Try not to eat them all at once!

CHEF ANNE'S
DRIED CHERRY & ALMOND
BISCOTTI

MAKES: 35 TO 50 · TIME: ABOUT 1 HOUR

Biscotti are traditional Italian cookies that you bake twice—they're super-hard and crunchy because they're meant to be dunkers. What I love about them is that you can flavor them any way you like. I love dried cherries and almonds (a killer combo!), but you can have fun swapping in other dried fruits, nuts, or spices if you want. Biscotti are the perfect dipping cookie—so whip up a batch and grab an espresso, some milk, or better yet, a glass of Vin Santo!

MISE EN PLACE

8 tablespoons (1 stick) unsalted butter, at room temperature

1 cup granulated sugar

2 large eggs, plus 1 white

1 teaspoon vanilla extract

2 cups all-purpose flour, plus more as needed

1 teaspoon baking powder

Pinch of kosher salt

Grated zest of 1 lemon

½ cup whole blanched almonds, toasted (see page 17)

¾ cup dried cherries

2 tablespoons turbinado sugar

1 Preheat the oven to 300°F.

2 In a large mixing bowl, combine the butter and granulated sugar and mix, scraping down the sides as needed, until light and fluffy. Beat in the 2 whole eggs one at a time, stirring to combine thoroughly after each addition. Add the vanilla.

3 Gently mix in the flour, baking powder, salt, and lemon zest. Stir until all the dry ingredients are fully incorporated. Fold in the almonds and cherries.

4 Line a baking sheet with parchment paper or a silicone mat. Divide the dough in half. On a lightly floured surface, roll the dough into two logs, about the length of the baking sheet, and place them on the prepared baking sheet.

5 Beat the egg white with 1 tablespoon water. Brush the logs with the egg wash, sprinkle them with the turbinado sugar, and bake for 30 minutes.

6 Remove the logs from the oven, transfer to a cutting board, and use a serrated knife to cut them into ½-inch slices—on the bias—while they are still warm (slicing them while warm will prevent crumbling). Keep the ends to nibble on while the other biscotti are baking.

7 Lay the biscotti back on the baking sheet and bake for another 10 minutes to toast and harden.

8 Let the biscotti cool and store in an airtight container.

Start dipping!

BLUEBERRY NECTARINE
CRISP

SERVES: 6 TO 8 · TIME: ABOUT 45 MINUTES

Anything with a crisp topping makes me a happy, happy girl. Crisps are homey and rustic and they make the most of whatever fruit is in season. When nectarines and blueberries are at the farmers' market at the same time, this combo is totally amazing. Crisps also work beautifully as individual portions or as one nice big one. I like to serve mine with lots of whipped cream or vanilla ice cream . . . mmmmm.

MISE EN PLACE

FOR THE FILLING

2 pints blueberries, picked through for stems and crushed berries

5 nectarines, peeled, pitted, and cut into 1-inch chunks

½ cup granulated sugar

Grated zest of 1 lemon

¼ cup cornstarch

FOR THE TOPPING

1¼ cups whole wheat flour

½ cup rolled oats

1 cup packed light or dark brown sugar

½ teaspoon cinnamon

Pinch of kosher salt

12 tablespoons (1½ sticks) unsalted butter, cold, cut into pea-size pieces

1 teaspoon vanilla extract

FOR THE FILLING

1 Preheat oven to 350°F.

2 In a large mixing bowl, combine the blueberries, nectarines, sugar, lemon zest, and cornstarch.

3 Place the fruit mixture in a wide, shallow baking dish (2 to 2½ quarts) or eight 1-cup ramekins.

FOR THE TOPPING

1 In a food processor, combine the flour, oats, brown sugar, cinnamon, and salt and pulse.

2 Add the butter and vanilla and pulse, pulse, pulse until the mixture looks dry and crumbly. Add 1 tablespoon water and pulse again until the mixture starts to come together. If the mixture still seems dry, add 1 more tablespoon water and pulse again. Sprinkle the topping over the blueberry mixture.

3 Bake for 25 to 30 minutes, or until the filling is hot and bubbly and the topping is crispy and nicely browned. Serve warm with whipped cream or ice cream.

Berry delicious!

ANNE ALTERNATE Apples, peaches, pears, plums, berries—you can substitute pretty much any fruit or combination of fruit that you like here. Have fun!

BREAD PUDDING

SERVES: 10 TO 12 · TIME: ABOUT 3 HOURS

This is my idea of fall and winter all wrapped up in a pudding dish! I take basic custard and ratchet it up by adding pumpkin and maple syrup. Then to keep it super-sexy, I use challah, which is a rich, buttery, and slightly sweet bread. This isn't your ordinary, everyday, bread pudding; this bread pudding is more like cake—and I like cake!

MISE EN PLACE

1 4-pound pumpkin, preferably a sugar pumpkin, or 3 cups canned pumpkin purée

2 cups heavy cream

¼ cup packed light or dark brown sugar

4 large eggs

1 cup REAL maple syrup

1½ teaspoons cinnamon

¼ teaspoon nutmeg

¼ teaspoon allspice

1½ teaspoons vanilla extract

1 tablespoon unsalted butter for greasing dish

1 loaf of challah, cut into 1-inch chunks (about 8 cups)

½ cup walnuts, toasted (see page 17) and coarsely chopped

½ cup dried cranberries or golden raisins

1 Preheat the oven to 375°F.

2 Cut the pumpkin into quarters, place it on a baking sheet, and roast for about 1 hour or until the pumpkin is fork-tender. Remove the pumpkin from the oven and let cool (this can be done a day or two ahead). When the pumpkin is cool enough to handle, peel off the skin, remove the seeds and guts, and purée the flesh in a food processor. If you're using canned pumpkin, skip this step.

3 Reduce the oven temperature to 325°F.

4 In a large bowl, combine the puréed pumpkin, heavy cream, brown sugar, eggs, maple syrup, cinnamon, nutmeg, allspice, and vanilla, and mix well to combine.

5 Butter a 9 x 13-inch baking dish well. Toss the bread, walnuts, and cranberries together in the baking dish. Pour the pumpkin mixture over the bread and let sit for 30 minutes.

6 Put the dish in the oven and bake for 50 to 55 minutes or until the custard is set.

Hey, punkin' puddin'!

ANNE ALTERNATE If you want to get really fancy, use cinnamon brioche or pound cake in place of the challah. Mmmmm . . .

STRAWBERRY-RASPBERRY SHORTCAKES

SERVES: 6 TO 8 · TIME: ABOUT 45 MINUTES

Shortcakes remind me of the ice cream socials we used to have in my small town when I was growing up. We always had strawberry shortcakes, but now I throw raspberries into my version to make them a little bit fancier and a lot more fun. I also make them free-form—by not using a biscuit cutter, I get cakes that look craggy and knobby, kind of like little toads. But they have a beautiful crumbly texture and act like sponges for the fruit juice without getting soggy. These are SOOOOO delicious that I can hoover a few of them in one sitting!

MISE EN PLACE

FOR THE FRUIT

1 pint strawberries, topped and quartered

1 pint raspberries

2 tablespoons sugar

Grated zest and juice of 1 orange

6 fresh mint leaves, cut into a chiffonade (see page 58)

FOR THE SHORTCAKES

1 cup all-purpose flour

2 tablespoons sugar

1½ teaspoons baking powder

Pinch of kosher salt

4 tablespoons (½ stick) unsalted butter, cold, cut into pea-size pieces

¼ cup heavy cream

½ teaspoon vanilla extract

1 pint vanilla ice cream, taken out of the freezer about 15 minutes before serving

FOR THE FRUIT

In a large bowl, toss together the strawberries, raspberries, sugar, orange zest, and orange juice. Let the mixture sit for at least 30 minutes to allow the fruit to release some of its juice.

FOR THE SHORTCAKES

1 Preheat the oven to 450°F.

2 In a food processor, combine the flour, 1 tablespoon of the sugar, baking powder, and salt. Pulse to combine.

3 Toss in the butter, heavy cream, and vanilla and pulse, pulse, pulse until the mixture comes together to form a rough ball; it should look fairly crumbly.

4 Line a baking sheet with parchment paper or a silicone mat. With lightly floured hands, form the dough into craggy-looking balls, a bit larger than golf balls. They should look a little like toads and DEFINITELY not be perfect. Place the balls on the baking sheet and squish each ball to flatten it some; sprinkle the balls with the remaining tablespoon of sugar.

5 Put the cakes in the oven and bake for 11 to 12 minutes, or until golden brown. Remove and let cool.

TO ASSEMBLE

1 Toss the mint with the fruit and stir to combine.

2 Cut the shortcakes in half equatorially, place the bottom halves on individual plates, and divide the fruit and juice among them. Place a scoop of ice cream on top of the fruit, replace the tops, and serve immediately.

Let's get shorty!

INDEX

Note: Page references in *italics* indicate photographs.

A

Almond
  Crust, Lemon Curd Tart with, 225–27, *226*
  & Dried Cherry Biscotti, Chef Anne's, 246
  Purée & Mushrooms, Braised Chicken Thighs with, 150–51, *151*
Anise Seed Cookies, Mom's, 224
Appetizers / first courses
  Calamari Noodles with Fingerling Potatoes & Black Olives, 64–65, *65*
  Escarole Salad with Walnuts, Pecorino & Pickled Onions, 73
  Garlic Steamed Mussels with Pimentón Aïoli, 66–67, *67*
  Grilled Pizzetta with Stracchino, Sausage, Arugula & Chili Oil, *70*, 71–72
  Grilled Porcini with Poached Egg & Parmigiano, 74–76, *75*
  Grilled Sea Scallops with a Watermelon Three-Way & Dandelion Greens, 80–81, *81*
  Grilled Shrimp with Chickpea Fries, Zucchini & Pine Nut Salad, 78–79, *79*
  Grilled Soft-Shell Crabs with Asparagus, Arugula & Spring Onion Salad with Aïoli, 82–83, *83*
  Heirloom Tomato Salad with Warm Goat Cheese, 77
  My Big Fat Chicken Soup, 94
  Oysters on the Half Shell with Prosecco "Sno-Cone," 86, *87*
  Parmigiano Flan, 95
  Pumpkin Soup with Allspice Whipped Cream & Fried Leeks, 88–89, *89*
  Raw Asparagus, Red Onion, & Pecorino Salad, 90, *91*
  Ricotta-Stuffed Zucchini Blossoms with Panzanella (a.k.a. Yummy Bread Salad), 68–69
  Roasted Beet & Many-Herb Salad, *92*, 93
  Spicy Chickpea Soup with Crispy, Crunchy Croutons, 84–85
  Sugar Snap Pea Salad with Crispy Prosciutto & Mint, 96, *97*

Apple
  & Olive Oil Cake with Sautéed Apples & Mascarpone, 232–34, *233*
  & Sweet Potato Hash, 214, *215*
Artichokes, Braised Baby, 204–5, *205*
Arugula
  Asparagus & Spring Onion Salad with Aïoli, Grilled Soft-Shell Crabs with, 82–83, *83*
  Parmigiano Flan, 95
  -Prosciutto Breadstick "Brooms," *44*, 45
  -Walnut Sauce, Tagliolini with, 121
Asparagus
  Arugula & Spring Onion Salad with Aïoli, Grilled Soft-Shell Crabs with, 82–83, *83*
  Parmigiano Flan, 95
  Raw, Red Onion, & Pecorino Salad, 90, *91*
  Tagliolini with Salsa Cruda & Ricotta Salata, 126, *127*

B

Bacon. See also Pancetta
  Corn, & Chili Crostini, 56, *57*
  Killer Mac & Cheese with, *140*, 141
  Sweet Corn, Burst Cherry Tomatoes & Arugula, Tagliatelle with, 125
Bean(s)
  Cannellini, with Pancetta & Rosemary, 194–95, *195*
  dried, cooking, 55
  Fava, Chanterelles & Spring Onions, 202, *203*
  Fava, Spring Pea & Ricotta Ravioli with, 130–31, *131*
  Grilled Shrimp with Chickpea Fries, Zucchini & Pine Nut Salad, 78–79, *79*
  Pasta Fagioli, 112, *113*
  quick soaking, 195
  Spicy Chickpea Soup with Crispy, Crunchy Croutons, 84–85
  White, Purée with Prosciutto, 54–55
  Yummy Lentils, 210
Beef. See also Veal
  Big Brown Braised Short Ribs with Horseradish, 158–59, *159*
  Dry Rubbed Bone-In Rib Eye (Just Good Stuff), 156, *157*

Polpetti Burgers, 163
Polpettini (Yummy Little Meatballs), *46*, 47
Spag & Excellent "Meatbawls," 122–24
Beet(s)
  Roasted, & Many-Herb Salad, *92*, 93
  testing for doneness, 93
Berries
  Blueberry Nectarine Crisp, 247
  Strawberry-Raspberry Shortcakes, 250–51, *251*
Black Bass, Seared Crispy-Skin, 183
Blueberry Nectarine Crisp, 247
Breading, for deep-frying, 51
Bread Pudding, Maple-Pumpkin, 248, *249*
Bread Salad, Yummy (Ricotta-Stuffed Zucchini Blossoms with Panzanella), 68–69
Breadstick "Brooms," Prosciutto-Arugula, *44*, 45
Broccoli Rabe
  Pesto & Sausage, Orecchiette with, *128*, 129
  Roasted Butternut Squash, & Pumpkin Seeds, Whole Wheat Pappardelle with, 132–33, *133*
Bruschetta, Tomato-Basil, 58
Brussels Sprouts
  Frizzled, with Pancetta & Walnuts, 206, *207*
  Slaw, 199, *199*
Burgers, Polpetti, 163

C

Cabbage, Braised, Stuffed with Sausage & Fennel, 167–69, *168*
Cakes
  Goat Cheese Cheesecake with Spiced Nilla Wafer Crust, 230–31, *231*
  Hazelnut, with Nutella Mousse, 228–29, *229*
Calamari Noodles with Fingerling Potatoes & Black Olives, 64–65, *65*
Caramel
  preparing, 237
  Salty, Tarallucci with, 244–45, *245*
Cauliflower
  Parmigiano-Crusted, with Garlic Dipper, 50–51

Sicilian, & Parsley Salad, Seared
  Red Snapper with, *180, 181–82*
Spice-Roasted, & Jerusalem
  Artichokes, 208, *209*
Cheese. *See also* Ricotta
  Chef Anne's Light-as-a-Cloud
    Gnocchi, 105–6
  Escarole Salad with Walnuts,
    Pecorino & Pickled Onions, 73
  Figs Stuffed with Gorgonzola &
    Walnuts, *34*, 35
  Goat, Cheesecake with Spiced
    Nilla Wafer Crust, 230–31, *231*
  Goat, Peperonata with, *38*, 39
  Goat, Warm, Heirloom Tomato
    Salad with, 77
  Grilled Pizzetta with Stracchino,
    Sausage, Arugula & Chili Oil, 70,
    71–72
  Hard Polenta Cakes with Taleggio
    & Cherry Tomatoes, 48–49, *49*
  Killer Mac & , with Bacon, *140*, 141
  Parmigiano-Crusted Cauliflower
    with Garlic Dipper, 50–51
  Parmigiano Flan, 95
  Pommes Chef Anne, *212*, 213
  Pork Milanese & Escarole Salad
    with Pickled Red Onions,
    Hazelnuts & Pecorino, 160–62,
    160
  Potato, Prosciutto & Fontina Cake,
    211
  Raw Asparagus, Red Onion, &
    Pecorino Salad, 90, *91*
  Super Creamy Cheeeeesy Polenta,
    198
  Tagliolini with Arugula-Walnut
    Sauce, 121
  Tagliolini with Salsa Cruda &
    Ricotta Salata, 126, *127*
  Zucchini & Parm Fritters with Spicy
    Tomato Sauce, 28–30, *29*
Cheesecake, Goat Cheese, with
  Spiced Nilla Wafer Crust,
  230–31, *231*
Cherry(ies)
  Dried, & Almond Biscotti, Chef
    Anne's, 246
  Juicy, Jammy, Jelly Tart, 240–41, *241*
Chicken
  Grilled, with Lemons & Dijon,
    146–47, *147*
  Liver Pâté with Balsamic Onions,
    36, *37*
  Rosemary & Lemon Roasted, with
    Gravy, 148–49
  Soup, My Big Fat, 94
  Thighs, Braised, with Mushrooms &
    Almond Purée, 150–51, *151*

trussing, 149
Chickpea
  Fries, Zucchini & Pine Nut Salad,
    Grilled Shrimp with, 78–79, *79*
  Soup, Spicy, with Crispy, Crunchy
    Croutons, 84–85
Chiffonade, method for, 58
Chocolate
  Dipper & Zeppole, 242–43
  Hazelnut Cake with Nutella
    Mousse, 228–29, *229*
Cookies
  Anise Seed, Mom's, 224
  Chef Anne's Dried Cherry &
    Almond Biscotti, 246
  Tarallucci with Salty Caramel,
    244–45, *245*
Corn
  Grilled, Bacon & Chili Crostini,
    56, *57*
  Sweet, Bacon, Burst Cherry
    Tomatoes & Arugula, Tagliatelle
    with, 125
Crabs, Grilled Soft-Shell, with
  Asparagus, Arugula & Spring
  Onion Salad with Aïoli, 82–83,
  83
Crostini, Grilled Corn, Bacon & Chili,
  56, *57*

D
Desserts
  Apple & Olive Oil Cake with
    Sautéed Apples & Mascarpone,
    232–34, *233*
  Blueberry Nectarine Crisp, 247
  Chef Anne's Dried Cherry &
    Almond Biscotti, 246
  Goat Cheese Cheesecake with
    Spiced Nilla Wafer Crust,
    230–31, *231*
  Hazelnut Cake with Nutella
    Mousse, 228–29, *229*
  Juicy, Jammy, Jelly Tart, 240–41, *241*
  Lemon Curd Tart with Almond
    Crust, 225–27, *226*
  Macedonia (My Super-Special Fruit
    Cocktail), 238, *239*
  Maple-Pumpkin Bread Pudding,
    248, 249
  Mom's Anise Seed Cookies, 224
  Pear Tarte Tatin with Shortbread
    Crust, 235–37, *236*
  Strawberry-Raspberry Shortcakes,
    250–51, *251*
  Tarallucci with Salty Caramel,
    244–45, *245*
  Zeppole & Chocolate Dipper,
    242–43

Dips and spreads
  Baked Ricotta with Rosemary &
    Lemon, 59
  Chicken Liver Pâté with Balsamic
    Onions, 36, *37*
  Mortadella Pâté, 26, *27*
  White Bean Purée with Prosciutto,
    54–55
Duck
  Breast with Dried Fruit & Vin Santo,
    152–53, *153*
  Confit & Bitter Greens, Chef
    Anne's Cheater's, 154–55
  Fat Potatoes, Crispy Crunchy, *218*,
    219

E
Eggplant Cakes with Ricotta, 43
Egg(s)
  Pasta Carbonara, 111
  Poached, & Parmigiano, Grilled
    Porcini with, 74–76, *75*
  poaching, technique for, 76
  Ravioli al'Uovo (Ricotta-Nestled
    Egg Yolk), 116–17, *117*
  Truffled Deviled, 32, *33*
  whites, whipping, 234
Escarole
  Salad with Pickled Red Onions,
    Hazelnuts & Pecorino, Pork
    Milanese &, 161–63, *162*
  Salad with Walnuts, Pecorino &
    Pickled Onions, 73

F
Farrotto with Lobster, Peas, Mint &
  Oregano, 138–39, *139*
Fennel
  Pollen, Brined Pork Chops with,
    170–71, *171*
  & Sausage, Braised Cabbage
    Stuffed with, 167–69, *168*
  -Tomato Sauce, Olive-Oil-Poached
    Tuna in, Spaghetti with, *118*,
    119–20
Figs Stuffed with Gorgonzola &
  Walnuts, *34*, 35
Fish. *See also* Shellfish
  fresh, buying, 182
  Halibut in Paper with Yummy
    Summer Veg, 184–85, *185*
  Seared Crispy-Skin Black Bass,
    183
  Seared Red Snapper with Sicilian
    Cauliflower & Parsley Salad, *180*,
    181–82
  Spaghetti with Olive-Oil-Poached
    Tuna in Tomato-Fennel Sauce,
    118, 119–20

Fish (continued)
Whole, Roasted, with Sliced Potatoes, Olives & Herbs, 186, 187
Flan, Parmigiano, 95
Fritters, Zucchini & Parm, with Spicy Tomato Sauce, 28–30, 29
Fruit. See also specific fruits
Dried, & Vin Santo, Duck Breast with, 152–53, 153
Macedonia (My Super-Special Fruit Cocktail), 238, 239

G
Garlic
Dipper, Parmigiano-Crusted Cauliflower with, 50–51
& Herb-Roasted Fingerlings, 217
Mashers, Loosey-Goosey, 216
Steamed Mussels with Pimentón Aïoli, 66–67, 67
Gnocchi
Chef Anne's Light-as-a-Cloud, 105–6
Spinach & Ricotta, with Fontina Fonduta, 134–35, 135
Grains
Chef Anne's Risotto-Without-a-Recipe, 136
Farrotto with Lobster, Peas, Mint & Oregano, 138–39, 139
Hard Polenta Cakes with Taleggio & Cherry Tomatoes, 48–49, 49
Risotto with Rock Shrimp, Lemon & Herbs, 137
Super Creamy Cheeeeesy Polenta, 198
Greens. See also Arugula
Bitter, & Duck Confit, Chef Anne's Cheater's, 154–55
Dandelion, & Watermelon Three-Way, Grilled Sea Scallops with a, 80–81, 81
Escarole Salad with Walnuts, Pecorino & Pickled Onions, 73
Pork Milanese & Escarole Salad with Pickled Red Onions, Hazelnuts & Pecorino, 160–62, 160
Spinach & Ricotta Gnocchi with Fontina Fonduta, 134–35, 135
Swiss Chard with Pancetta and Baby Turnips, 196, 197

H
Halibut in Paper with Yummy Summer Veg, 184–85, 185

Hazelnut(s)
Cake with Nutella Mousse, 228–29, 229
Pickled Red Onions & Pecorino, Pork Milanese & Escarole Salad with, 160–62, 160
Herbs
dried, note about, 17
Many-, & Roasted Beet Salad, 92, 93
Horseradish, Big Brown Braised Short Ribs with, 158–59, 159

J
Jelly Tart, Juicy, Jammy, 240–41, 241
Jerusalem Artichokes & Cauliflower, Spice-Roasted, 208, 209

L
Lamb
Rack of, Crusted with Black Olives, 172, 173
Shanks, Braised, 174–76, 175
Lemon Curd Tart with Almond Crust, 225–27, 226
Lentils, Yummy, 210
Liver, Chicken, Pâté with Balsamic Onions, 36, 37
Lobster, Peas, Mint & Oregano, Farrotto with, 138–39, 139

M
Macedonia (My Super-Special Fruit Cocktail), 238, 239
Maple-Pumpkin Bread Pudding, 248, 249
Meat. See also Beef; Lamb; Pork; Veal browning and braising, 176
Meatballs
Polpettini (Yummy Little Meatballs), 46, 47
Spag & Excellent "Meatbawls," 122–24
Mortadella Pâté, 26, 27
Mushroom(s)
& Almond Purée, Braised Chicken Thighs with, 150–51, 151
Chanterelles, Fava Beans & Spring Onions, 202, 203
Grilled Porcini with Poached Egg & Parmigiano, 74–76, 75
Oyster, Chips, 42, 42
Sausage & Pancetta Stuffed, 40–41, 41
Wild, Ragù, 107
Mussels
buying, 67
Garlic Steamed, with Pimentón Aïoli, 66–67, 67

N
Nectarine Blueberry Crisp, 247
Nuts. See also Almond; Hazelnut(s); Walnut(s)
toasting, 17

O
Olive(s)
Black, Rack of Lamb Crusted with, 172, 173
Sliced Potatoes, & Herbs, Whole Roasted Fish with, 186, 187
Stir-Fried Marinated, 31
Onion(s)
Balsamic, Chicken Liver Pâté with, 36, 37
Bucatini all'Amatriciana, 114, 115
Cipolline Tempura with Aïoli, 52–53, 53
Pickled, Walnuts & Pecorino, Escarole Salad with, 73
Pickled Red, Hazelnuts & Pecorino, Pork Milanese & Escarole Salad with, 160–62, 160
Oysters
buying and shucking, 87
on the Half Shell with Prosecco "Sno-Cone," 86, 87

P
Pancetta
and Baby Turnips, Swiss Chard with, 196, 197
Pasta Carbonara, 111
& Rosemary, Cannellini Beans with, 194–95, 195
& Walnuts, Frizzled Brussels Sprouts with, 206, 207
Parsley Salad & Sicilian Cauliflower, Seared Red Snapper with, 180, 181–82
Pasta
Bucatini all'Amatriciana, 114, 115
Carbonara, 111
Chef Anne's Light-as-a-Cloud Gnocchi, 105–6
cooking and serving, 104
Dough, Chef Anne's All-Purpose, 102–4
Fagioli, 112, 113
Killer Mac & Cheese with Bacon, 140, 141
Orecchiette with Broccoli Rabe Pesto & Sausage, 128, 129
Ravioli al'Uovo (Ricotta-Nestled Egg Yolk), 116–17, 117
Spag & Excellent "Meatbawls," 122–24

Spaghetti with Olive-Oil-Poached Tuna in Tomato-Fennel Sauce, *118,* 119–20

Spinach & Ricotta Gnocchi with Fontina Fonduta, 134–35, *135*

Spring Pea & Ricotta Ravioli with Fava Beans, 130–31, *131*

Sweet & Spicy Sausage Ragù, *108,* 109–10

Tagliatelle with Bacon, Sweet Corn, Burst Cherry Tomatoes & Arugula, 125

Tagliolini with Arugula-Walnut Sauce, 121

Tagliolini with Salsa Cruda & Ricotta Salata, 126, *127*

Whole Wheat Pappardelle with Roasted Butternut Squash, Broccoli Rabe & Pumpkin Seeds, 132–33, *133*

Wild Mushroom Ragù, 107

Pâté

Chicken Liver, with Balsamic Onions, 36, 37

Mortadella, *26,* 27

Pear Tarte Tatin with Shortbread Crust, 235–37, *236*

Pea(s)

Lobster, Mint & Oregano, Farrotto with, 138–39, *139*

Spring, & Ricotta Ravioli with Fava Beans, 130–31, *131*

Sugar Snap, Salad with Crispy Prosciutto & Mint, 96, 97

Peppers

Peperonata with Goat Cheese, 38, 39

Piccolini (little bites)

Baked Ricotta with Rosemary & Lemon, 59

Chicken Liver Pâté with Balsamic Onions, 36, 37

Cipolline Tempura with Aïoli, 52–53, *53*

Eggplant Cakes with Ricotta, 43

Figs Stuffed with Gorgonzola & Walnuts, *34,* 35

Grilled Corn, Bacon & Chili Crostini, 56, 57

Hard Polenta Cakes with Taleggio & Cherry Tomatoes, 48–49, *49*

Mortadella Pâté, *26,* 27

Oyster Mushroom Chips, *42,* 42

Parmigiano-Crusted Cauliflower with Garlic Dipper, 50–51

Peperonata with Goat Cheese, 38, 39

Polpettini (Yummy Little Meatballs), 46, 47

Prosciutto-Arugula Breadstick "Brooms," 44, 45

Sausage & Pancetta Stuffed Mushrooms, 40–41, *41*

Stir-Fried Marinated Olives, 31

Tomato-Basil Bruschetta, 58

Truffled Deviled Eggs, 32, 33

White Bean Purée with Prosciutto, 54–55

Zucchini & Parm Fritters with Spicy Tomato Sauce, 28–30, *29*

Pizzetta, Grilled, with Stracchino, Sausage, Arugula & Chili Oil, *70,* 71–72

Polenta

Cakes, Hard, with Taleggio & Cherry Tomatoes, 48–49, *49*

Super Creamy Cheeeeesy, 198

Polpettini (Yummy Little Meatballs), 46, 47

Pork. *See also* Bacon; Prosciutto; Sausage

Bucatini all'Amatriciana, *114,* 115

Chops, Brined, with Fennel Pollen, 170–71, *171*

Milanese & Escarole Salad with Pickled Red Onions, Hazelnuts & Pecorino, 160–62, *160*

Mortadella Pâté, *26,* 27

Polpetti Burgers, 163

Polpettini (Yummy Little Meatballs), 46, 47

Rockin' Porchetta with Fall Veggies, 164–66, *165*

Spag & Excellent "Meatbawls," 122–24

Potato(es)

Chef Anne's Light-as-a-Cloud Gnocchi, 105–6

Crispy Crunchy Duck Fat, *218,* 219

Fingerling, & Black Olives, Calamari Noodles with, 64–65, *65*

Herb- & Garlic-Roasted Fingerlings, 217

Loosey-Goosey Garlic Mashers, 216

Pommes Chef Anne, 212, *213*

Prosciutto & Fontina Cake, 211

Sliced, Olives & Herbs, Whole Roasted Fish with, 186, *187*

Sweet, & Apple Hash, 214, *215*

Poultry. *See* Chicken; Duck

Prosciutto

-Arugula Breadstick "Brooms," 44, 45

Crispy, & Mint, Sugar Snap Pea Salad with, 96, 97

Potato, & Fontina Cake, 211

White Bean Purée with, 54–55

Pumpkin

-Maple Bread Pudding, 248, *249*

Soup with Allspice Whipped Cream & Fried Leeks, 88–89, *89*

R

Raspberry-Strawberry Shortcakes, 250–51, *251*

Ravioli

al'Uovo (Ricotta-Nestled Egg Yolk), 116–17, *117*

Spring Pea & Ricotta, with Fava Beans, 130–31, *131*

Recipes

Anne-isms used in, 20

basic pantry items for, 19

herbs for, 17

kitchen tools for, 18

prep work for (*mis en place*), 16

reading ahead, 15

seasoning with pepper, 17

seasoning with salt, 16–17

spices for, 17

tasting as you go, 16

toasting nuts for, 17

Red Snapper, Seared, with Sicilian Cauliflower & Parsley Salad, *180,* 181–82

Rice

Chef Anne's Risotto-Without-a-Recipe, 136

Risotto with Rock Shrimp, Lemon & Herbs, 137

Ricotta

Baked, with Rosemary & Lemon, 59

Eggplant Cakes with, 43

Ravioli al'Uovo (Ricotta-Nestled Egg Yolk), 116–17, *117*

& Spinach Gnocchi with Fontina Fonduta, 134–35, *135*

& Spring Pea Ravioli with Fava Beans, 130–31, *131*

-Stuffed Zucchini Blossoms with Panzanella (a.k.a. Yummy Bread Salad), 68–69

Risotto

with Rock Shrimp, Lemon & Herbs, 137

-Without-a-Recipe, Chef Anne's, 136

S

Salads

Escarole, with Pickled Red Onions, Hazelnuts & Pecorino, Pork Milanese &, 160–62, *160*

Escarole, with Walnuts, Pecorino & Pickled Onions, 73

Salads (*continued*)
    Heirloom Tomato, with Warm Goat
        Cheese, 77
    Parsley, & Sicilian Cauliflower,
        Seared Red Snapper with, *180,
        181*–82
    Raw Asparagus, Red Onion, &
        Pecorino, *90, 91*
    Roasted Beet & Many-Herb, *92, 93*
    Sugar Snap Pea, with Crispy
        Prosciutto & Mint, *96, 97*
Sausage
    & Broccoli Rabe Pesto, Orecchiette
        with, *128, 129*
    & Fennel, Braised Cabbage Stuffed
        with, 167–69, *168*
    & Pancetta Stuffed Mushrooms,
        40–41, *41*
    Ragù, Sweet & Spicy, *108*, 109–10
    Stracchino, Arugula & Chili Oil,
        Grilled Pizzetta with, *70, 71*–72
Scallops, Sea, Grilled, with a
    Watermelon Three-Way &
    Dandelion Greens, 80–81, *81*
Seafood. *See* Fish; Shellfish
Shellfish
    Calamari Noodles with Fingerling
        Potatoes & Black Olives, 64–65,
        65
    Farrotto with Lobster, Peas, Mint &
        Oregano, 138–39, *139*
    Garlic Steamed Mussels with
        Pimentón Aïoli, 66–67, *67*
    Grilled Sea Scallops with a
        Watermelon Three-Way &
        Dandelion Greens, 80–81, *81*
    Grilled Shrimp with Chickpea
        Fries, Zucchini & Pine Nut Salad,
        78–79, *79*
    Grilled Soft-Shell Crabs with
        Asparagus, Arugula & Spring
        Onion Salad with Aïoli, 82–83, *83*
    mussels, buying, 67
    oysters, buying and shucking, 87
    Oysters on the Half Shell with
        Prosecco "Sno-Cone," *86*, 87
    Risotto with Rock Shrimp, Lemon &
        Herbs, 137
    shrimp sizes and counts, 79
Shortcakes, Strawberry-Raspberry,
    250–51, *251*
Shrimp
    Grilled, with Chickpea Fries,
        Zucchini & Pine Nut Salad,
        78–79, *79*
    Rock, Lemon & Herbs, Risotto
        with, 137
    sizes and counts, 79

Slaw, Brussels Sprouts, 199, *199*
Soups
    Chicken, My Big Fat, 94
    Pumpkin, with Allspice Whipped
        Cream & Fried Leeks, 88–89, *89*
    Spiced Chickpea, with Crispy,
        Crunchy Croutons, 84–85
Spices, notes about, 17
Spinach & Ricotta Gnocchi with
    Fontina Fonduta, 134–35, *135*
Squash. *See also* Zucchini
    Maple-Pumpkin Bread Pudding,
        248, *249*
    Pumpkin Soup with Allspice
        Whipped Cream & Fried Leeks,
        88–89, *89*
    Roasted Butternut, Broccoli Rabe
        & Pumpkin Seeds, Whole Wheat
        Pappardelle with, 132–33, *133*
Stock, preparing, 85
Strawberry-Raspberry Shortcakes,
    250–51, *251*
Sweet Potato & Apple Hash, 214, *215*
Swiss Chard with Pancetta and Baby
    Turnips, 196, *197*

T
Tarallucci with Salty Caramel, 244–45,
    245
Tarts
    Juicy, Jammy, Jelly, 240–41, *241*
    Lemon Curd, with Almond Crust,
        225–27, *226*
    Pear Tarte Tatin with Shortbread
        Crust, 235–37, *236*
Tempura, Cipolline, with Aïoli, 52–53,
    53
Tomato(es)
    -Basil Bruschetta, 58
    Bucatini all'Amatriciana, *114*, 115
    Burst Cherry, Bacon, Sweet Corn &
        Arugula, Tagliatelle with, 125
    Cherry, & Taleggio, Hard Polenta
        Cakes with, 48–49, *49*
    -Fennel Sauce, Olive-Oil-Poached
        Tuna in, Spaghetti with, *118*,
        119–20
    Heirloom, Salad with Warm Goat
        Cheese, 77
    Oregano & Pine Nuts, Stewed
        Zucchini with, 200, *201*
    Pasta Fagioli, 112, *113*
    for pasta sauces, 120
    Sauce, Spicy, Zucchini & Parm
        Fritters with, 28–30, *29*
    Seared Red Snapper with Sicilian
        Cauliflower & Parsley Salad, *180,
        181*–82

Spag & Excellent "Meatbawls,"
    122–24
Tagliolini with Salsa Cruda &
    Ricotta Salata, 126, *127*
Truffled Deviled Eggs, 32, *33*
Tuna, Olive-Oil-Poached, in Tomato-
    Fennel Sauce, Spaghetti with,
    118, 119–20
Turnips, Baby, and Pancetta, Swiss
    Chard with, 196, *197*

V
Veal
    Polpetti Burgers, 163
    Polpettini (Yummy Little Meatballs),
        46, *47*
    Shanks, Whole Braised, 177–78
    Spag & Excellent "Meatbawls,"
        122–24
Vegetables. *See also specific
    vegetables*
    Fall, Rockin' Porchetta with, 164–66,
        165
    Perfect Green Veg...Every Time,
        192, *193*

W
Walnut(s)
    -Arugula Sauce, Tagliolini with, 121
    & Gorgonzola, Figs Stuffed with,
        34, *35*
    & Pancetta, Frizzled Brussels
        Sprouts with, 206, *207*
    Pecorino & Pickled Onions,
        Escarole Salad with, 73
    Watermelon Three-Way & Dandelion
        Greens, Grilled Sea Scallops
        with, 80–81, *81*

Z
Zeppole & Chocolate Dipper, 242–43
Zucchini
    Blossoms, Ricotta-Stuffed, with
        Panzanella (a.k.a. Yummy Bread
        Salad), 68–69
    Halibut in Paper with Yummy
        Summer Veg, 184–85, *185*
    & Parm Fritters with Spicy Tomato
        Sauce, 28–30, *29*
    & Pine Nut Salad, Grilled Shrimp
        with Chickpea Fries and, 78–79,
        79
    Stewed, with Tomatoes, Oregano &
        Pine Nuts, 200, *201*
    Tagliolini with Salsa Cruda &
        Ricotta Salata, 126, *127*